KARSTEN MASSEI, born 1963, first studied political science in Berlin, but then decided to train as a special needs teacher in Switzerland. Since then he has taught in a special needs day-school in Zurich, where he also lives. Besides this work, Karsten Massei gives courses and seminars on the practice of supersensible perception, spiritual enquiries into bees, and on the nature of animals, trees and medicinal plants. He also increasingly studies pedagogical themes.

D1212554

CHILD OF
THE COSMOS

Strengthening Our Intrinsic Being

Karsten Massei

Translated by Matthew Barton

TEMPLE LODGE

Temple Lodge Publishing Ltd.
Hillside House, The Square
Forest Row, RH18 5ES

www.templelodge.com

Published by Temple Lodge 2022

Originally published in German under the title *Das Wesen des kosmischen Kindes, Ein Weg zur Stärkung der Individualität* by Futurum Verlag, Basel, Switzerland, 2020

A CIP catalogue record for this book is available from the British Library

ISBN 978 1 912230 90 7

Cover by Morgan Creative
Typeset by Symbiosys Technologies, Visakhapatnam, India
Printed and bound by 4Edge Ltd., Essex

Contents

Introduction

This book takes its starting point from an unpleasant experience—blindness to one's own being. Our self-knowledge is extremely limited and superficial. What do we know about our true nature? Bridling at this unpleasant experience seems to be of no use, for we meet it time and again, involuntarily of course.

While we may intuit our divine nature, it is soon apparent that we know little about it. And we are equally inept and unpractised in relating to our own shadow and wounds. In relation to our own intrinsic being, we can easily feel like a child, a beginner, a learner: a long journey awaits us before we can fully understand ourselves.

*

The content of this book lies in the interplay, and tensions, between the human individual and the nature of our inner child. Both of these reveal themselves to unbiased self-observation. Both are enigmatic. They appear before our inner eye but without explanation of their significance and task. Their enigmatic nature can be very troubling to us, but can also lead us to attend more thoroughly to ourselves, to listen more carefully.

The individuality and the inner child are complex entities. It is because they are directly related to each other that it makes sense to concern ourselves with them both. They have many faces, are contradictory, and our enquiries therefore have to be patient and persistent if we are to understand them. Both are deeply connected with our destiny and with the earth and the cosmos. They stand there as question and enigma, and yet they are a wellspring of strength and healing.

*

As our insights into our own nature deepen, our frailties, deficiencies and inner wounds become increasingly apparent. A point comes when they can no longer be ignored, when we can no longer avoid meeting them freely and openly. The being of the inner child, and her sister, the cosmic child, want to educate the individual to become inwardly truthful and authentic. These beings wish to teach every person to become aware of their own divine nature, but without shutting their eyes to inner wounds. Honest engagement with the traumas and vulnerabilities of our own soul is the only thing that will enable the individual to attain a true picture of their own personality.

*

Our era demands of each of us that we learn to handle our forces and powers with care. We quickly come up against our limits. If we have a sensitive disposition, as many do, there is all the more danger of over-extending ourselves. On the one hand, sensitivity summons diverse and distinctive experiences that nourish our soul and spirit and help us mature and develop. On the other hand, sensitivity or empathy is often coupled with a thin skin. Deep experiences that delve into the intrinsic qualities of phenomena must often be paid for with a great vulnerability which is not always easy to cope with.

In this context many questions arise. Nowadays, whether they wish it or not, a great many people have to battle with these questions. They make efforts to protect themselves, necessitated by their great susceptibility to what happens around them. In fact, the phenomena of our time require everyone today, really, to develop this gesture of self-protection. This book aims to help explore these questions.

*

At this point it should be stressed that the quest to find oneself is far too sacred and significant an undertaking to rely upon external authorities, and this applies too, of course, to the thoughts gathered here. This book will fulfil its aim if it stimulates readers to pursue their own autonomous search for self-knowledge.

*

To achieve our own experiences in this realm we must of course develop certain perceptual techniques and soul capacities. Besides the ordinary senses there are other, inner senses, which facilitate insights into supersensible reality. Meditation serves to awaken our attention so that these other senses can be developed and schooled. The insights they make possible allow us to gain deep knowledge of our own being. Such discoveries are always bound up with the individuality of the investigator. This should not disconcert us. We should not think that this means losing the necessary objectivity. In fact, a truth can only become meaningful and effective if it passes through a person's individual nature. Otherwise it remains abstract, something arbitrary I can either believe or not. Only what I myself have experienced can usefully serve my life.

*

The third section of this book gathers together meditations that are intended to help readers inwardly engage with some of its contents. It is fine to refer to them as you read, that is, to practise them before getting to the end of the book.

I
THE LIFE OF THE INNER CHILD

1
Transformations

Mostly we dream, after all, living in a state governed by inner images, assumptions, opinions and convictions. We are given up to this state of mind for many hours of the day. Because of it we tell ourselves that we possess something that enables us to find our way through life. It is like swimming in a big river. But nowadays this state of being no longer sustains us, no longer suffices: it awakens resistance, anger, anxiety, even repugnance. We know that we wish to get beyond it, for it weakens and erodes us. From it arise decisions that constrict us, that expose us, that lead us astray. We no longer trust ourselves. We actually shy away from acting because we are far from certain whether the basis of our decisions and deeds is a sure and sustaining one, whether it accords with us.

*

We are still a long way from self-possession. For a while now we have been pursuing many paths through many lands and epochs, trying to be one with ourselves. But what has been our experience thus far? As yet, we seem to know so little about ourselves. And we scarcely understand the name by which we refer to ourselves every day. Who can claim to know the 'I' that they call themselves? Who even knows how they came to this name? If this is even unclear, how can we think that we are not the greatest mystery to ourselves? And yet thinking such a thing is difficult, it makes us restless, nervous, dissatisfied. If we go down this road, how will the questions ever end? We prefer to have a quiet life. Yet this quiet is deceptive and false. We know this. But everyone carries on as if this were for the best: they become masters in suppressing their unknowing. And yet by this means, surely, no one succeeds in coming to terms with their deeper reality.

*

This is compounded by the fact that we often appear like strangers to ourselves. Then we have only the vaguest idea of what we should be doing. Time stands still, we wait and do not know for what—for something that will not arrive, however, until we bestir ourselves. But how and in what direction, toward which goal? And who am I to myself anyway? What a strange, fragmented, contradictory being! Either we quickly forget such moments again or they do not fade. They stay with us. Then it seems to us as if we carried a flaw, a taint in us. We cannot get rid of it, and it broods within, stirring up mischief and difficult to deal with.

*

Then we feel how much work still needs doing. It is as if we stood at an edge and gazed into a void, feeling it to be far too big for us and yet belonging to us. Each of us still casts very long shadows. They fall into the void, where they seem to belong, they merge with it. That's what happens with our own soul's darknesses. Who dares look at them without turning away? Yes, self-knowledge is a laborious business, and sometimes a dreadful one. We avoid it because the shame we feel about ourselves becomes unbearable. And who wants to lose their self-respect? Who can endure their own shadows? We are all beginners at this.

*

At certain moments of our life significant turning points come, above all ones that lead inward. Often they are elicited by outward events which expand into personal crises. Then we learn as we fall. Doubt, fear, powerlessness become our teachers. The shadows we have trusted before lose their power over us. Intimations surface. Signs become visible, showing us the important things we have overlooked until now. We have pursued certain paths, may even have chosen them freely, have acted, have realized ideas that now reveal themselves as ones we were wrong to submit to, were wrong to give precedence to instead of what lives in us, what we bear within us, as our deep existential wishes.

This takes its revenge and reveals itself as crisis—yet slowly, once the worst is over, we awaken again, come into new strength and arrive at new insights. We feel an unaccustomed gratitude for the disaster that struck us, the hand we were dealt. Without it, the wheel in which we were imprisoned would simply have gone on revolving. We would have run on, hurried on, stumbled on. Now new ways of seeing awaken—ones that in most cases we already knew of or at least had an inkling of, but which we adroitly pushed away.

*

Crises are transformations, the shedding of skins. To our surprise we recognize that there are other ways of looking at life beside the one we have cultivated. The crisis was necessary. It served to broaden our view, but also our feelings and knowledge. We become aware of the responsibility we have toward our own development. We have lived at odds with ourselves, have not taken ourselves seriously enough: our own view of things, our own needs, our own feelings, thoughts, wishes, longings, also our own fears and anxieties. We have passed ourselves by. Now we feel that our strength has increased, our ability to see ourselves and our circumstances, our tasks, other people, in the right light. The crisis helps us to behold and endure more and more of ourselves. To accept ourselves.

*

Crises are anything other than new. Each of us has passed through many of them. We know these states from our previous lives. Every such state is a sign, a beginning, a gateway we must pass through to come nearer to ourselves. A crisis is always the beginning of a path inwards. A crisis cannot help but shake us up and make us look at ourselves and the world differently. Through crisis a light germinates—a light we know well; that we knew before the crisis already but did not wish to believe in. It is the light of a path that goes inwards. Fundamentally it is the light of the mystic path, of the path of initiation into the secrets of the inner life of the soul and existence.

2
Inward paths

And so we walk onward. In earlier times people were prepared for this journey, and accompanied in it, by priests and shamans. They had to undergo an extensive schooling, full of privations. They were led from one stage of initiation to the next through inner and outer crises. The aim was for them to come ever more to resemble their spiritual being, and in doing so grow part of a particular tradition which their teachers represented and preserved.

Nowadays these ancient temples, these forms of initiation, have lost their justification. And this is connected with the fact that human individuality has strengthened to a point where it can no longer submit to these old forms of initiation. Instead of obeying particular rules, or another human being, our task is to learn to obey ourselves. We live in a time when a person can no longer follow others as used to be the case. To do so would mean to deny and ultimately negate ourselves. Other capacities now come to replace obedience and compliance; among other things these involve learning to hearken and attend to oneself, to one's own inner voice of wisdom. We can no longer acquire wisdom by self-subjection but only by turning to the living sources of our own being. Wisdom is in everyone. This has always been known. In our time, seeking it means pursuing our own unique path. One hears suggestions, tips and advice of all kinds, and these can be very helpful. But we do not have to accept them blindly and bind ourselves to them, which would mean overlooking our own wellsprings.

*

In our time it is right for people to explore their inner mystery independently. It is right for us to discern and reject anything that seeks to exert power over us in some way. This includes all ideas, dogmas, forms of thinking and habits of thought. The mystery and wisdom in our own nature will be able to shine only a dull or weak light if we think that our own development is dependent on certain thought patterns, forms of thinking, ideologies or worldviews. These must inevitably be held at arm's length if we wish to gain a spiritual perception of ourselves, of our own sacred being. Otherwise there is a danger that we will lose ourselves. What others have thought and deemed true can never be binding on us. It can inspire us, can counsel and empower us, but no more than that. It should never become part of our own identity. Otherwise these thought forms replace what only we ourselves can determine.

The task for people in the modern era is to learn and practise authenticity. This work awaits all of us. What we seek are our own wellsprings—those which are ours alone, which we need not share with anyone because they are an expression of our unique and intrinsic destiny.

*

Yet veils shroud our own soul, and confuse our gaze, impenetrable veils that make it hard to look inward. The true countenance or the true countenances of the soul are concealed. We sense the masks through which the soul struggles to be perceived.

If only we could simply set off, depart as we do for an outward journey! Pack a bag, put on our coat, pick up the key, and off we go. The soul withdraws from such spontaneous attempts. It makes itself scarce. You get a sense that it sets conditions for the person who seeks to discover it, ones that are not easy to fulfil.

*

Novalis speaks of these inward journeys, of wanderings through the realms of soul, when he writes in his 'Pollen' fragments:

> We dream of travelling through the universe: but surely the universe lies within us? We do not know the depths of our spirit. The mysterious path leads inward. Within us or nowhere is eternity with its worlds, the past and the future. The outer world is the shadow world, casting its shadows into the realm of light. At present, certainly, it seems so dark within us, lonely, formless; but how different it will appear when this darkness passes and the shadow body is shifted aside. Then we will delight more than ever, for our spirit has lacked what nourishes it. [no. 16]

Reading such words, we recognize in astonishment that in fact the soul is a land where all manner of things occur. *'Travelling through the universe'*: what should we think of this? Novalis speaks of light and shadows, though more of shadows. What concepts and experiences do we ourselves have of this? What does darkness mean, what does light mean for the soul? Yes: 'At present, certainly, it seems so dark within us, lonely, formless…'. This is true. Things seem dark, very dark when we direct our gaze inward into the soul. We look into a realm from which has vanished all the light we know so well as the light of the sun in the outer world. But besides such moments there are others, special and rare ones, when we feel that our own soul is more than merely a realm of shadows. There is more, much more there. When we listen inwardly, we find a luminosity, a delicate, tentative light that is hard to describe. It has to be admitted that we have only a very elementary and therefore meagre knowledge of it. And yet we can feel this mysterious light or luminosity which, at the same time, seems to harbour a mysterious power. It remains through all the states familiar to us, which we can inhabit—it does not disappear but shines despite all darkness. Yet it is not easy to hold fast to. What we know of it is still very uncertain and nebulous.

3
Voyage into the soul

Where the soul is concerned, exploration or travelling inward means, paradoxically, letting go: shutting your eyes and shedding all daily thoughts, all memories, worries, anxieties; stopping for a moment what we otherwise do so unreservedly and persistently when we allow ourselves to be carried forward in the stream of our own thoughts. As such, that is fine and there is nothing wrong with it. But this stream hinders our exploration of the realms of our own soul.

Swimming in this flowing ocean of thoughts, without being able to step out of it—since its power urges us onward, carries us with it, and allows no cessation— we might as well give ourselves up to it and not worry, for it is not always helpful to try to defend ourselves against its surge. It is better to surrender, simply. For this streaming flow will eventually recede. It may turn in circles a few more times, but eventually subsides, grows tranquil. If we do not feed it with any new matter, it will starve. And as soon as this stream grows more peaceful, quieter and at last grows insignificant, we feel ourselves becoming the inhabitant of our own house. And we can also help ourselves with meditations, with powerful words or phrases which we read and allow to act upon us until they have grown great and resound in our whole soul. This soothes the little, loud and meddlesome thoughts. They can dissolve into these great words, and find healing there. Helpful likewise are the 'I AM' phrases from the Gospel of John, which strengthen our forces of awareness, and make it easier for us to give ourselves up to the truth of the soul.

*

When Novalis says that *'the shadow body is shifted aside'*, he no doubt means that we let ourselves fall into the soul while retaining our consciousness. By doing so we succeed in pursuing the secret tracks inscribed in the soul upon its wanderings. These lead us through the spheres of the night as if through the realms which the soul enters after death. As yet we know far too little about ourselves to admit narrow self-conceptions. Perhaps we are the sparks of a great fire which we do not see because we think the sparks are everything. Certainly, courage is needed to enlarge our thinking. This courage is necessary because we have been taught the habit of believing the opposite—specifically, that every individual is insignificant. Each person passes away irrevocably when they die. The earth, we are told, is a grain of dust in the cosmos. But who can know this? What presumption to assert it. If we set about exploring our inner being, we eventually arrive at a point where we find that such a view does not encompass the whole of our nature. We discover an indescribable breath within us, a grandeur and nobility, for which words scarcely suffice. We must therefore be careful not to be presumptuous or arrogant. We can feel that our own being cannot be circumscribed. We become attentive to the mysterious traces that have inscribed themselves in the soul on its long travels.

*

The soul appears deep and unfathomable as an ocean. It is hazardous to set forth and surrender ourselves to it, for in doing so we leave sure ground behind us, exchanging this for something that is not easy to trust. We never lose a sense of our own soul as harbouring dangers for which we are not equipped. We sense, after all, that in our inwardness we are without end, full of alien waters, unknown islands, wild creatures and dangerous adventures. What we know of this inner ocean appears insignificant compared to what we do not know. We contain worlds within us of which we do not even have faint inklings. I possess only the first beginnings of myself. There is much more there that is inaccessible to my consciousness.

What surges to the shore, wave upon wave, is the secret speech of the gods, its outermost fringes. They speak in the wind, in the clouds. They live there. We hearken to their humming, their ringing and thunder. They speak in the elements, in the light, in water, in fragrances, in storm and rain. They speak within me too, but through a different veil there, through the veil of my soul, through the power of my attention, through my compassion, dignity, my fear and envy. These are traces and gestures of their lofty nature. These are the signs they inscribe when they reveal themselves within us. For good reason they speak only thus, in signs, for they are sublime and would be too strong for us if we felt and saw them entirely.

*

Our departure needs to be well prepared. We should equip ourselves properly, for the journey will fail if we take with us restlessness, worries, burning thoughts which we cannot cast aside. The inner ocean is wild and only obeys sailors who can establish a mood of harmony in their feelings and thoughts. The ocean of the soul hearkens only to a state of inner tranquillity, otherwise it will prove master of ship and seafarer. All too often the soul cannot breathe for bodily tension. The body holds it spellbound to a degree that will not allow it to discern itself. Breathing exercises and other physical practices can be very helpful here, as can imaginations in which we place ourselves in a calm, pleasant and beautiful place. Then thoughts, worries and memories shed all the relentless reverberations of outer occurrences. Their flames grow softer, their demands less insistent. Over time everyone finds their own means of soothing what hinders the seafarer from leaving harbour to discover the purity and multiplicity of the great inner ocean.

The path to our inner being certainly passes through stillness. And it is a key task for people today to come to know and master this tranquillity. We cannot dispense with it if we are to behold our true nature.

*

During this voyage, we encounter pictures which life has inscribed in the soul. Memories surface, long-gone experiences, each unique and unrepeatable. They are present. And I *am* them, they are the pillars of my inner life. Or sisters of my soul, friends, companions.

They change; some fade, others intensify. Some keep surfacing, unasked, as if in admonition. Some we yearn for, others we await with alarm. But they all have one thing in common: they are the foundation upon which we rest or from which we step away at each moment of our life. Without them we would never find our tranquillity. Consciousness runs along their rail, for through them we experience ourselves as a being with a history. As we trace the pictures we find within us, we are also always searching for the sphere that safeguards our own self. They carry me. They make me known to myself. They lend strength and duration. And they are the signs of my presence upon the earth. I can hold to them when I ask myself how I have grown and developed and become what I am.

*

In the course of life we gather ideas about ourselves that can hinder us since they interfere with our self-quest. Taking them with us as we set sail upon the ocean of our own soul can easily lead us astray. I have certain views of myself. I think I know who I am, what my abilities are, what I am unable to do. I stand before myself in a very particular way—but this must not limit or confine me. I must always ensure that I do not allow the ideas, judgements and opinions I have about myself to rule me. We are very self-critical, but this can undermine the spontaneity of our perception of our individual nature and being. I myself limit this. But to find myself I need to retain the ability to encounter myself anew at every moment. Whatever suppresses spontaneity distances me from myself. It is one of the hardest of all things to try to perceive oneself directly. And the reason for this is that we seek support from pillars that stand close to untruth. We take our lead from phrases such as, 'I am too easy to impress' or, 'I am too self-preoccupied' or, 'My career is important to me' or, 'I have no opinions of my own' or, 'I always feel at fault'. Such phrases, and others, are true as long as we see them as transitional states, but untrue if we allow them to harden into fixed dogmas. As long as we acknowledge ourselves to be changing and developing, perception of our own being can remain spontaneous and immediate, for then we can look through the veil of our own assumptions and ideas.

4

The inner child

As we proceed inwards, into the depths of our own soul, things grow dimmer and darker. But that is only one aspect. They also become brighter. We will speak about the darkness later, but here we will start with the light. In our childhood beginnings, we lived in a special light, really in a great dream. Things and events had a magic which the child we were regarded as natural; once we are adults they seem to be something we no longer dare give ourselves up to fully. For the child everything is pervaded by flooding life: the world speaks to us, usually very clearly. Children simply lend everything their own voice, speak to trees and animals as if they were people. They live in continual companionship, receptive to marvels; and it is easy for them to arrange everything to fit their desires: the table becomes a house, the shoe a boat, and the little doll or play figure they themselves, ready to embark on wonderful adventures. As we look back, this dream may seem unreal. But this is only because we do not so easily find our way back to it. In our childhood experience this dream was full of magical power, a place where we unwound the thread of our own life, feeling and thinking our way into everything, in sympathy with the life of all things and creatures. The child encompasses everything, feels exalted and mighty— something that all too easily fades away in later life.

The child plays all day long and does not think of stopping. In this way she incorporates the outer world, makes it her own and adapts it to herself. She brings with her the gift of play and transformation. Her inner world too, which she carefully unfolds and elaborates as she plays. Play is happiness. In playing the child masters the world and herself.

Puberty puts an end to this dream, though only provisionally, for if one wishes one can go on dreaming it. Even if we have been rudely awoken and have only a few memories reaching back to this dream state, it is not lost for ever. It can never really end. But we have to learn to dream again, consciously now. The soul of the child still bears within it the happiness and good fortune of its life in an unsullied state, fresh and inviolate. We have journeyed on and have received wounds. Play has been driven out of us. But this does not mean that we cannot recapture it. This does not mean that it will not descend upon us again.

*

This child is still alive, although hidden. In the stillness of the soul. But we can meet her—we need only wish to. It is easier than we might think. Really she is waiting for us to seek her. We can lend her our ears and listen to her. We can ask her questions. We can ask her how she is or what she wants to tell us. If we find the necessary tranquillity and patience, she will start to speak. At first very quietly, almost inaudibly. But when she notices that we are listening, her shyness fades. She begins to smile and shine upon us, begins to tell us things. Perhaps to begin with she speaks of cheerful, happy experiences then soon also of other, more important things—of what is most vital for her.

Yes, our inner child tells us what it means to play. Through play we learn that nothing is unimportant. Everything is full of significance, we need only be attentive enough. Nor can we miss any opportunity—that's the second thing to learn. Nor can we be wrong: mistakes are preposterous, an illusion in fact. For when we play we simply are, nothing more nor less. We can learn from our inner child to touch, hold and see the things of life in a different light, and also allow them to touch us, and touch upon us, differently.

She tells us other, still more serious things as well. She says that we are awakening very slowly to the meaning which the earth has. We are only at the beginning. The earth's true momentousness is so far only dawning tentatively. We do not yet have a gaze that can see the earth in its full significance. And she tells us still more: she says that she feels very safe in the being, the bosom of the earth. The child is in good hands, in the hands of Mother Earth. Yes, the earth keeps safe the human being's childlike, virginal soul, which dwells within a body in which no harm can come to it.

*

These and other observations arise when we give ourselves up to the ocean of our soul. Within it live beings whom we only know when we encounter them. With time it becomes apparent that the inner child is the messenger of another, greater being, the being of the earth. She speaks of this being as of her own mother. Voyages through our own soul always lead us to impressions, experiences and glimpses of the motherly being of the earth. Our inner child lies in her lap and is kept safe by her.

If we wish, we can wander through the meadows of our soul and so gain deep impressions of the being of the earth. Then we feel that the earth is our soul's mother. There may be others, but she is certainly one of them. She gives birth to us. But this means that, in her protection, we can slowly grow, step by step, without any pressure. Always questing further, always thinking we have too little, are too little, and always wanting more, she calls to us: You lack nothing, you lack only attention to what is already present. She does not urge us to be other than we really are. In her gaze we do not have to be anything at all, for we are sufficient already. But we are also aware that we do not yet know ourselves at all. We have not yet followed to the end all the intricate paths that reveal to us who we are.

*

On our wanderings through the archetypal mother-realms of our own soul, a further insight can dawn. We recognize that the earth conceives the human being even before conception by the bodily mother. First the womb of the earth opens her spiritual organism and receives the soul of the person who is to be born on earth. Only then can it be conceived by the mother who brings it to physical birth. The child in play still seems to know this. She plays with the earth, with the elements, with water, flowers, stones but also with light, shadows, animals, with day and night and with the stars as with brothers and sisters. In play she still carries within her the echoes of this greater conception.

*

Related to this is our feeling that the earth speaks with the human soul. Yes, she speaks with it continually. In doing so the earth draws the soul's attention to what is essential and indispensable, to all that is all too easily forgotten. She speaks quietly, her signs and messages often suddenly appear, often also seem inconspicuous and enigmatic, for the earth not only conceives the human soul, but also lives within it throughout our lives. She draws attention to herself in subtle nuances, slight motions, delicate perceptions. In doing so she lays aside the power and strength intrinsic to her. She speaks almost inaudibly, for otherwise what she says would be too strong and overpowering for our mind. To hear her messages we have to know the way in which she speaks with us. We have to adjust ourselves to her, to her delicate communications, if we wish to learn from her.

*

The nature of the inner child is very mysterious. But to encounter her is an occurrence that we do not so easily forget, for here we meet a being that we very certainly are, as we can feel precisely, but that surpasses what we have hitherto understood, known and perceived of ourselves. That she is bound up with the being of the earth is only one aspect. She is also bound up with our own individuality, with the part of it, in fact, that is still beyond our own capacity of perception. As an individual being—or we can also say, as a divine being—we are more than we can as yet comprehend. We are still on a quest for ourselves. We know only a part of our being. From our inner child comes the prompting not on any account to regard this part as the whole individual, for otherwise we are separating ourselves from the best in us. Our inner child beholds our entire, complete being, something we find very hard to perceive. This is because we are too bound up with what we call the sensory world. The being of the inner child is free of such constraints. She can turn her gaze both to divine and earthly worlds without becoming entirely engrossed by either.

5

The world of the gods and the self

The being of the inner child, in our era, faces very particular conditions and circumstances which will be characterized in the next few chapters.

Since primordial times, gods have held sway upon earth. The Ancient Persians, Egyptians, Greeks and Celts revered them and prayed to them, adopting from them the order according to which they lived. The idea that they merely imagined the existence of these deities is a presumption of the modern era, derived from an outlook that seeks to discredit the idea of supersensible worlds as a misguided fantasy. This in turn is based on a rationality that over-looks the human capacity to perceive tangible realities in worlds of spirit. But in every age there have been people who could demonstrate that they possessed such capac-ities. And this remains true today. We can even say that spiritual experiences are by no means uncommon in our time. There are many who testify to them. Encounters with the divine world are nothing exclusive, reserved only for certain groups or individuals. Such encounters are part of the everyday life of many people.

*

We can see that individuals today, through their own, direct experiences, are able to gain true and significant insights at the threshold of the world of spirit. They can recognize the meaning of sleep or of death. Many people have capac-ities that enable them to acquire such insights by their own means. In doing so they are not adhering to prevailing worldviews and religions but learn rather to acknowledge their own capacities of perception and to trust in them. A range of different methods of meditation exist for this. In a stance of contemplation we can gain answers to burning questions. For a long time now it has not been necessary any more to depend on others, on outer teachings or dogmas. We can trust in the answers we ourselves discover without relying on receiving them externally. This gesture of self-empowerment is a significant characteristic of our time.

The gods have not vanished, therefore, for they are intrinsically ageless. It is just that human beings are finding new ways to approach them. Experience shows that the idea of the 'world beyond' being barred to us is an unfounded rumour. It is here amongst us, and even—however alarming a thought—it is within us, a part of our being in fact, as it always has been.

*

Our encounter with the world of the gods, with the divine, spiritual world, surpasses all accounts to be found in literature, and all ideas that we may have formed of it. This encounter occurs very gradually, over years, over many years and lives. In most ways it is unexpected. Sudden and very intense experiences can surface: perceptions, visions that seem strange and alien, whose meaning only becomes apparent with time. Their meaning, in fact, does not always reveal itself at the same time as the visionary experience, and then it is necessary to wait, to proceed calmly, staying centred in oneself.

Often, to begin with, we lack understanding of what we thus perceive in the supersensible world. We do not know so clearly how we should interpret what we behold. Only with time do the sources we draw from and the beings with whom we interact reveal themselves. Initially we lack words and concepts that would explain this new world. Those we possess feel pale and feeble in regard to these experiences or perceptions. This can be unsettling, leading to many questions and troubling doubts. Only later, as more experiences accumulate, does the darkness begin to brighten.

*

There is also something good in the fact that we are initially confused. The path we are pursuing belongs only to us. No one else travels with us and we must rely on ourselves. It may seem odd that every single person in the world should have their own path into the spiritual world. But over time it becomes apparent that this is so. We can feel like the man in Franz Kafka's parable 'Before the Law'. Coming from the country, he waits for many years in front of a doorway before which stands a guardian who prevents him from entering. Only shortly before he dies does he ask the guardian of the doorway why no one apart from him has sought entry there in all the years.

> The doorkeeper sees that the man is at the point of death, and bellows at him to make sure his failing hearing still catches his words: 'No one else could gain entry here, for this doorway was meant only for you. I'm going to shut it now.'

This is macabre and somehow desolate. But the tale contains a true insight: I have my own unique path that no one else can follow. It is intended for me alone. Only I stand where I do, and no one else.

No one can take another's place. The feeling arising from this insight is still strange and discomforting to us. We do not let ourselves quite believe it, for it makes clear to us what divides one person from another. I am not the other, he is not I. Nor can I be he. We can make the effort of imagination to slip into another's skin, to take on their body, voice and life. Yes, we can imagine this, but it only reveals more clearly what separates us from one another. The other I, his other qualities, presents a boundary that cannot be overcome. Each person is their own distinct and unique being.

*

Such experiences arise as we approach the threshold of the divine world. Recognizing what is ours shows us how different the other is, and how different we are from them. Here an abyss opens that initially seems unbridgeable. That the other person's nature is alien can even oppress us. But this leads us to approach the world of spirit with care and caution since we have to learn, first, to deal with the abyss.

Loneliness lies in wait at the threshold to the world of spirit and belongs to it. Our own path opens a chasm which we only gradually come to acknowledge. Our connection with others increasingly feels one of loneliness. Their nature seems to change by virtue of the fact that I enter into a different relationship with myself.

But this does not have to remain so. It is just that the new forms of community have not yet dawned. They need time. In the meantime, states of deep loneliness can arise. But there is light within them. If we sharpen our perceptions we can feel this. There is a germ here of a new commonality.

*

We can ask who it was that imbued me with the belief that I should trust external authorities in fundamental matters of existence, life and destiny. It is sobering to feel within oneself the chains that come from this belief, which hamper me from seeing that my questions, already, draw on pre-existing answers. It is the answers that instigate our questions. The questions draw our attention to answers that have long existed and rest in us like seeds that wish to grow. I live my way towards my answers. They are within me and I will not find them outside myself.

Alongside this is the fact that nothing in the world can, after all, force me to oppose the view of another. I can listen and understand, but I do not have to reply. There is no need at all to feel challenged, and I don't even have to judge what I hear. I can simply attend, first of all, to what happens to what I have heard and absorbed. What I hear continues on its way. It settles within me, moves, moves me. I can observe this. And what I observe in this way will tell me enough. If I get angry about a view that someone expresses, or erupt in enthusiasm and jubilation about it, I am still at a stage of dependency. I am surrendering to the power of appraisals, views and judgements that are not mine.

In Kafka's legend of the doorkeeper, the man from the country allows himself to be intimidated by the guardian. He trusts in his words:

> If you are so keen to do this, feel free: try to enter despite me forbidding it. But don't forget I am powerful. And I am only the lowest doorkeeper. From room to room stand others, each more powerful than the other. I myself cannot endure the sight even of the third.

And so he stays where he is, in front of the gateway. The guardian makes such an impression on him that he spends his whole life waiting to be granted entry. The man from the country does not believe in himself, does not even seem to know such a thing is possible. He knows only the outer path, has only a dim inkling of the inner one—for otherwise he would not wait there as he does until his life is over. He shows no trace of capacity to acknowledge this dim inkling.

The man from the country fails in his quest. But why? There are many answers to this question, perhaps as many as there are readers of this parable. He fails because he has too little trust in himself, or because he is obedient, or because he has no self-belief. But he also fails for another reason: because he does not make the most of the encounter that presents itself to him. It does not even occur to him that this is worth doing. He feels no impulse to make the most of it or do justice to it. Basically, he behaves like a fool, uncertain and naïve. He relies on the appearance before him without looking into it further, without seriously exploring it further. Ultimately, he robs himself of what belongs to him.

6
The death-pangs of a time that's past

A great deal in public life today that surfaces in such threatening and feverish forms, and tries with such furious efforts to impress and dominate us, is nothing other than the death-pangs of an old world. To think that battle is still a viable approach is to misread the signs of the times. Prevailing ideologies and worldviews have long since exhausted themselves in battling and destroying each other. A great deal of energy and effort has been spent on accentuating the differences between different groups, races and religions. It is a deeply shameful thing that human beings have directed forces of destruction against other human beings. It is becoming ever clearer that ignorance, hatred, revenge and destructiveness are not the signs of strength but of weakness. They are admissions of the weakness of thinking that violence and destruction are legitimate and viable tools in human society; they show us deficiencies that should no longer be the sources of our action. They are signs of an inability to perceive and acknowledge the dignity and inviolability of other people.

What matters is no longer the differences between different religions, worldviews, ways of life and opinions but of what they hold in common. The tendency to focus only on differences is the expression of a cramp-like lack, a weakness that makes people try to define themselves in opposition to an adversary or enemy, seeing themselves as superior, and battling to destroy the other. Whether as a group or an individual, if we still need opponents and enemies to strengthen the sense of our own identity, this merely demonstrates a lack of maturity, autonomy and independence.

*

Criticizing and being criticized is something deeply familiar to us. We know what it feels like to be shamed, condemned and cursed, but also to shame, condemn and curse. We too have fought, wounded, killed and murdered. It is time, at last, to leave all this behind us. We can decide that this will end now. It is completely unnecessary to keep repeating these experiences—they always rise up against the one who cannot let go of them. There are always worse consequences for the one who wilfully harms another. Our soul no longer endures injuring others. This is to do with the fact that responsibility for our actions is increasingly passing to us. We are increasingly accorded our own self-responsibility. The gods deem us worthy of taking ever more responsibility for ourselves.

The decision to refrain from all exercise of power and force, the effort to transform gestures of opposition, criticism and battle, is a decisive step. It is an inner deed, one undertaken by our inner being. It is high time for this. Let us talk about it with one another. For communal life, the life of society, it is important to gain clarity together about power games that we still indulge in. Only this can help ripen a decision to relinquish them.

*

As we saw, the other is becoming stranger to us. An abyss divides people. Each individual is increasingly thrown back on themselves. They must increasingly relinquish outer supports. For this reason, convictions, ideologies and ideas that were previously sure foundations for us lose their justification. Their tendency to ignore the needs, experiences and path of the individual is becoming ever more unsustainable. They negate the individual in a way that means we can no longer uphold or abide by them. They mediate forms of life and thinking we can understand but to which we do not have to subordinate ourselves. Otherwise, in appropriating us, they would merely shroud our own individuality and rob us of it. They obscure the light of our divine and sacred being like a curtain shutting out sunshine.

It is interesting to study the conflicts still alive today between different religions and worldviews, but they no longer touch upon our inmost being. They are oriented to something that is now long outmoded. For someone witnessing them today, they appear empty and effortful. Such battles are illusory. They no longer revolve around anything substantial or essential—which is, rather, the intrinsic human being, our unique individuality, germinating in a way that makes all outer conflicts and battles appear shallow.

It is no longer important for the various religions and worldviews to fight each other but to begin instead to unite; and to do so out of the strength that lives in each individual. The important thing is to seek the uniting element by means of which all separate human beings can turn toward one another in a gesture of reconciliation.

*

The question now is what will fill the empty space hitherto occupied by the disputes between different groups of people, countries and religions? If we feel our way into this question, we can notice that the being of the human individuality is taking the place of people as groups. Before our inner eye the significance of the other person appears now as a key category for the future.

The individual person is always also a member of various groups that each make their particular contribution to individual identity. We have a gender, are part of a family, a village, a town, a social class, a political group, a nation, a period in history. But these factors become ever less determining for the individual who becomes aware of themselves as a unique entity. This does not mean they are unimportant: they create the living context in which the individual develops and comes into their own. But this milieu no longer makes us what we become. Today it is becoming ever more abstract and insubstantial so that it grows ever less possible to unite our identity with it. The figure who, instead, appears in ever more clarity, is the other person, their being, their secrets and their relationships. As the light of human groups fades, the light of the individual human being begins to shine forth ever more strongly.

*

What has so far preoccupied us points to a concern with practising a particular art, the art of meeting. Otherwise we will stay far too isolated, behold only what we already know and judge by standards we bring with us. We are novices in this art. But we can certainly sense that if we do not practise this art we will not cease to injure the earth. Our souls will not perceive the realms of the high deities and beings. We will never learn to understand the other person in their own truth. Meeting always also means making the most we can: of each opportunity, of the gifts of the other, of their wisdom, experience and power to heal. Meeting is a social art and the prerequisite for a capacity to discern other worlds, other people but ultimately also ourselves, our own true being. The social art is the archetypal art, the seed from which all else grows. It is to this that we will now turn.

The mysteries of the other

For everyone who engages with the mysteries of another person, doing so signifies an astonishing experience: you meet a unique world, a country entirely distinct and original. Within every person lies a reality intrinsic to them alone. Each of us is only the one we are and no other.

In addition, each person consists of layers leading from outwardly perceptible ones to ever more inward, invisible dimensions. Our external being always contains pointers to the next layer inward and this enables us to 'read' someone, to understand them. They reveal themselves in images that are directly perceptible, in which the effects of inner, hidden worlds make themselves manifest. A person's inner worlds reveal themselves in the sensory pictures of their outward existence. I behold this person when I consider their outward life, their biography and its events. But this means that I must develop a specific sense to intuit from these outward signs of a person's biography, behaviour, gestures, appearance and bodily form, something of the hidden worlds of their intrinsic being. Reading the script of another person's life is a skill fundamental to the art of social interplay and co-existence.

And we have to know these hidden worlds exist, and possess their own laws that are made manifest in their own way. It would be presumptuous to expect these laws simply to reveal themselves. But we can prepare ourselves to perceive them. To be able to wait for, and await, what lies hidden within is the essence of the art of meeting. It is in fact the right of every human individuality, and really of any and every entity, even plants and animals, to reveal themselves in the way that accords with them.

*

Reading another person is a kind of dreaming, although one where we retain our waking mind, and intensify it, rather than falling asleep. We dream into the sign language of another person. Without judgement. We listen, feel our way into them, let ourselves fall. We admit the impressions, feelings and experiences we receive from the other into our own soul, allowing them to resonate there in their own way and multiply. We open ourselves to freely receive the other's look, voice, gestures, appearance, handshake, life story, letting these spread in us like the ripples around a stone that falls into a calm lake. Over time the lake absorbs these ripples and undulations and unites with them. In the same way, the signs of the other unite with our own soul.

But we must not become impatient and do violence to this script by subjecting it to an outward interpretation. Let it convey itself without us analysing it, for otherwise it cannot unfold its life. Let us allow these signs their own rhythms.

Without judgement and over-hasty anticipation we can observe these signs as they sink into our soul, becoming aware of the traces they leave: light trails, sacred reverberations. We can hearken attentively to these echoes in us, conveyed as sounds, images, feelings, thoughts and insights. Every falling calls forth an ascending stream, and the sacred being of another person announces itself here in the echo rising within us. But we do not raise ourselves above the other, nor subordinate ourselves to them either. We stay entirely within the gesture of discernment. Our attention is focused on the realm of the soul in which the signs utter their meaning without us needing to do anything.

Accordingly, the spiritual individuality of the other touches us as this person themselves desires. We can feel that what we learn about them accords with what the person wishes to reveal of themselves. This approach ensures that we do not learn more than the spirit being of the other wishes us to know. This being remains safe and intact because we allow it not to reveal more of itself than it wants to.

The picture of the other that emerges in this way can be experienced as an enlarged, thus complementary picture to what we learned of them and knew of them before. It enlarges the picture we wrongly assumed to be the person in their entirety. This enlarging picture includes the aspect of the person that will never find its full expression in a single biography. Yet it comes to indirect effect as the spiritual seed out of which a person leads their life.

*

Now this picture of the other that we receive in this way is never finished once and for all. It is always only a beginning. It would run contrary to its nature for us ever to come to an end of it. But that is precisely what matters here, for it is a picture received from life's spiritual reality. What happens does not happen according to the measure and dictates of the one in whom it occurs. Through this picture the other speaks in a way that surpasses what we can experience with them in our meeting on the physical plane. Albeit only in a first, shy look, we behold the mysteries of the other. We do not behold their whole secret, for who could think they could perceive another in that way? But we behold the aspect they allow us to see. Each person retains the entirety of their mystery for themselves, for only they may disclose it.

*

In our quest we have arrived at an important point. In receiving a first and perhaps only faint and delicate impression of a person's whole being, which unites their physical appearance and their biography with its complementary image, thus their spiritual entelechy, we enter a sphere in which the divine being, that every person is in their original nature, shines forth. That we are gods can become a direct certainty at such moments. We behold another person in their divine semblance, in their identity with the divine being that they are and with which they will one day reunite. We come into the presence of another person in a way that allows us to perceive that we are gods.

If we take this seriously, we can come to feel united with the other in a way that only emerges if we go beyond the signs and forms of earthly life. What unites us is naturally not independent of our life on earth and yet is by no means limited to it. We are divine beings who, by virtue of our divine nature, relate to one another above and beyond earthly conditions. As gods, the divine world is open to us in so far as we can meet one another in a realm beyond earthly forms of life. The earth is not the sole sphere in which we meet. We lead a life as gods but also one as individual beings upon earth.

*

If I now faintly behold the light of the sacred being of another person, I also always behold myself. We have common sources that in this way become discernible. I and the other are my wellsprings. In no way can I dispense with those of the other if I am not to lapse into narrowness. The other's being discloses part of Creation to me, a part that could not be revealed without them. Each person can only become whole through others.

I feel a breath of this future and festive state when I manage to become receptive to the complementary, cosmic being of the other. I achieve this when I fall quiet. The deeper my silence, the clearer this being can appear before me.

*

The end of the path lies in darkness. The goal is more than nebulous. We do not yet fully know the one toward whom we are working our way. But we know that we cannot pursue this path alone. We need other people, friends, companions. And they need us. We can only pursue the path towards ourselves together. The I and the We are interleaved. The one is always founded on the other. Without the You, the I goes astray, as does the We without the I.

This becomes apparent whenever someone experiences a serious crisis. Where our customary inner props collapse, a void gapes open, and we start to fall headlong into catastrophe. The inner stability that would be needed to endure this void and this falling, thus to steady ourselves again upon our own foundations, is only slowly maturing. The chasms that open cannot be bridged without the help of others. When we are accepted by another who does not judge us, has no expectations, who listens, a power shines into our soul that helps to arrest our fall. The home that was lost, that we had to relinquish, we experience through another. During the time when we take leave of ourselves, we can rely upon someone else.

Human beings are strong foundations and possess a special healing strength. Not all have this to the same degree of course, but none can be without it.

To the degree that we develop our individuality, we need to be able to rely on other people increasingly. True friends become ever more indispensable. It is not true that we merely become stronger as we develop our individual nature; we also become ever more vulnerable and in need of protection. The paths to the gods, and to the divine being that we are ourselves, lead only through our friends.

*

The meeting with the other is always also a meeting with their inner child, whom we encounter as soon as we meet them. We can sharpen our sense of the nature of the other person's inner child. To perceive her we need the same mood of soul which leads to us experiencing our own inner child. We will need to refrain from our previous opinions and judgements about the other. At the same time we attune to their higher, intrinsic being. The child only shows herself when we lay aside all outer standards and measures and acknowledge only those which the other person brings forth from themselves. The inner child is a sensitive creature. She reveals herself only when she feels a desire for truth living in the gaze directed toward her human being. We do not approach the truth of the other through judgements, assumptions or opinions. But when we become aware that truth's wellspring lies in the other, that it lives there, then it can reveal itself through the inner child.

To feel or perceive the inner child of the other is truly a sacred deed. We cannot call her forth but only gratefully receive her.

We will discover that the nature of the inner child can be very different in different people. The age of a person, too, affects her nature.

The inner children of two people unite as soon as these people develop deep mutual understanding and trust. They are very much interwoven when two people are in love. Attentiveness and esteem for the other, tenderness and also erotic attraction, enable the inner children of two people to converse with each other. They participate in our mutual respect, honour and love, which give them significant help to grow and mature. When we perceive how the being of the other lives within us, the being of their inner child always also lives in us. We can feel how this gives rise to an enhancement of our own capacities.

8

Individual gifts and the community

The community must not curtail or limit the freedom of its members, for otherwise it loses its strength and wellspring. It must do all in its power to enhance this freedom. Finding and practising ways and forms that enable communities to follow these premises is of great importance for the future. Otherwise the opposition already at work between communities and the individual will grow ever more irreconcilable.

To seek these forms and ways addresses a deep need in people today. We desire to realize our individuality, but we also know that it would wither if it could not unfold within a community of other people, all of whom also wish to develop their individuality. Both—community and individual—are an indispensable source of development for each other.

It makes sense for a person to offer to others what they achieve or attain. To develop at the cost of others makes no sense. Someone who takes only for themselves what they achieve steals from the community its bread of life. But in the same way, the community that pays no heed to nurturing and supporting every individual, shuts off the wellspring essential to each person. If the community really succeeds in nurturing individuals, the bond uniting self and community is strengthened. If individuals give their gifts to the community (though without sacrificing themselves in the process), they help to develop it in turn, each in their own way. Thus a community is on the one hand formed and enlivened through each of its members, and on the other, the community creates for each of its members the protective membrane that each of us needs for our individual development.

*

Developing respect for what happens in the social sphere is essential for the organs of the community, and for the individual. The organs of the community, and all its individuals, must practise precise perception of what is actually happening within their sphere. Without unsullied perception a free interplay between the community and the individual cannot really happen. The community with its organs and individuals, must continually seek to wrest true pictures from sometimes dramatic and turbulent occurrences. They must learn to read what occurs as signs whose interpretation and understanding is indispensable for the life of the community. Reality tends to deceive us when we try to observe it. Social processes in particular can easily conceal their true countenance, their true meaning and message. We have to work in a rigorous way to avoid being deceived. This is to do with the complexity of social relationships but also with the limited perspective of the observer.

*

We have to be very aware that the truth is often painful since it shows us, as observers, that we are not simply free and independent. We easily tend to have preconceived opinions and form premature and unjust judgements. This is poisonous to true and unsullied pictures of social relationships. The ability to judge, that is, to gain a picture that corresponds to actual occurrences and situations in a community, is one we still need to develop. We should therefore be very cautious about judging. Reaching sure appraisals is a path that requires consciousness. It is not enough to judge; it is equally important to be clear about how well-founded the judgement is.

Judgements can only have a healing and conciliatory effect if the person they relate to can at the same time regard themselves with respect. Making judgements also involves keeping a respectful focus upon oneself. By doing so, we safeguard the social process and the people involved. If we cannot summon the discipline necessary to gain a true picture of our own nature, we do not 'deserve' to form a view of another person. We need to be able to apply to ourselves the same rigour that we apply to another. Otherwise untrue pictures emerge.

Gaining clarity about these processes is one task of modern and future-oriented communities.

*

In the same way that the community has obligations to the individual, so the individual also has obligations to the community. The community requires loyalty of individuals, which the latter can only muster if they are in accord with the goals pursued by the community. They must be able to say yes to the aims embodied by the community. If this is not the case, an individual will only *pretend* loyalty. Likewise, the way in which community members relate to one another must accord with the expectation and ideas of the individual, who has certain expectations of how one should handle differences of opinion, how to reach solutions and, above all, how to relate to power structures. Subjection to someone in authority is a gesture which no longer has any place in a modern society, nor in an enterprise, government body or state institution. This creates a climate of humiliation and uncertainty, one unworthy of modern human beings.

*

Each member of a community bears responsibility for the judgements and pictures living within it. The cleaner and truer they are, the freer will be mutual dialogue and discussion, and the easier it will become to reach shared decisions. It is a prime task of the community to maintain clean, true pictures of its members. A community that is aware that such work is an important foundation of the collaborative endeavour in which its members engage, will enhance its strength and resilience. The members of the community will be able to perceive that living substance is created through the community, a social substance. The freer that members of a community wish to be, the stronger becomes their need to pay heed to the work of forming this social substance.

*

Where communities make the freedom of the individual sacrosanct, a distinctive spiritual substance develops through human co-existence. This can only arise in free communities and disappears with the emergence of power structures to which members subordinate themselves. This substance can be discerned in the forming of spiritual ties and threads between members. There is harmony between the aims and goals of the community and the freedom of its individuals. Here one can perceive a healing stream living amongst people and also radiating from the community. This social substance encompasses and envelops the community, protects its members' activities and aims, and shines outwards.

9
Communities and clairvoyance

In the Introduction we referred to the fact that we are living in an era when people's receptivity to phenomena beyond the veil of the senses is markedly increasing. Human consciousness is becoming ever less restricted to the sense world, and therefore it intimates, feels and also perceives this world beyond the veil ever more clearly as an essential reality. We can speak of a natural clairvoyance of the modern soul, distinct from any conscious inclination toward the divine world that a person may pursue. Natural clairvoyance is not bound up with faith or religiosity but develops completely independently of these.

For many people nowadays premonitions are a matter of course. They have clear impressions of future events and can inwardly prepare for them. At certain moments they read others' thoughts, can feel how they feel or know how they are about to respond. They have encounters with those who have died, or with elemental beings or angels.

These intimations or perceptions represent a special challenge for them. They do not always know how to deal with them. Their sensitivity or receptivity is often interpreted as over-sensitivity, and their reactions, to which they must often resort to protect themselves, as lack of empathy. Their experiences, and the behaviour that results from them, meet with little understanding. When they speak of their perceptions this often elicits indignation, fear and anxiety. It can reach the stage when people question or doubt their perceptions, and this does not make it easy for them to gain a positive relationship to their own capacities.

*

Perceptions that go beyond the sense world also signify that those who have them develop a new relationship with sense reality. As soon as they find that the sense world is no longer the whole of truth and reality, it too becomes a new world for them. They move through it differently. What happens around them and with them acquires different meaning. They will give ever less credence to things that before seemed to them clear and self-evident. What they regarded as true now shows itself, to their surprise, to be appearance, and what they thought was illusion reveals its deeper truth.

But they too undergo a major change. Along with the growing sensitivity to things that occur around them they become altogether more vulnerable, indeed fragile. They feel themselves affected by many things in a way that no longer allows them to take a neutral stance toward the pain they suffer. This can be unsettling. They can experience others' feelings as their own, and often need time to free themselves from these again. If they are no longer able to detach themselves from these influences, this will lead to difficult emotional states.

*

Communities that wish to live out of modern impulses must acknowledge developments of these kinds. This means they must reckon with the fact that the human soul is undergoing a significant transformation. On the one hand the human individuality feels itself incapable of accepting an imposed, external authority; on the other, experiences surface which show us that the sense world is quite certainly pervaded by a supersensible, spiritual reality.

A community—thus a family, social institution, company, local council, school or university, marriage or friendship—can only be regarded as contemporary if they take sufficient account of these developments.

We cannot begin to resolve the social problems that arise if no account is taken of the transformations currently occurring in the human being. Our social tasks can only be addressed if due attention is given to human development. Ignoring this will only exacerbate the problem since paths taken to resolve it miss the core of the issue. Only if we pay heed to the new qualities of soul appearing today in very individual ways in every human being, will we find keys to tackling the great challenges of the age.

Because of what younger people, especially, now bring with them, such challenges face those, above all, who have a leading role in a project, training, institution, company or a local authority. Their position of responsibility means they must engage with these new capacities. It is easy to misjudge a situation when we meet in another something that seems alien and enigmatic, and does not accord with the order of things to which we are accustomed.

II
THE WOUNDED AND THE COSMIC CHILD

1

Responsibility toward the earth

It is deeply shameful that human beings impair and injure the earth's inviolate, natural purity. They wound the earth. They disdain the body that sustains them and gives them life. Through our conduct, the earth and the entities living upon it arrive at a state that deeply disturbs and unsettles anyone who perceives their afflictions with wakeful heart. The suffering of the earth and of the creatures that inhabit it points fundamentally to the afflictions of humankind. What drives us to violate the earth and disdain it, as has happened for a good while now, exposes a trait of our own. What we do to the earth is a stain, a deep flaw, of our own, which shows what a predicament we find ourselves in. Only someone who is wounded can wound in turn. We can feel how we lose our own dignity when we ignore the dignity of the earth.

In the Western world the earth and its creatures have largely been seen as objects of endless exploitation and profit. Technical developments of the past two centuries, and the potential they have unleashed, have led humankind down this mistaken road. The earth is regarded as a 'production factor' that primarily serves to increase our quality of life, wealth and security.

This is an outmoded view. The earth itself refutes it. Numerous current phenomena are bringing home to us the fact that we must review and revise our relationship to the earth, must change our conduct towards it and our way of life. This has led to a new, germinal sense of responsibility towards the earth. Realities and actual conditions are forcing us to question the convictions, habits and actions that have led to such consequences for the health of the earth and her creatures. We can no longer act as if our ways of being have no ecological impact.

*

In past eras people had a sense of their responsibility towards the earth. They felt and experienced the planet as a gift of the gods. They felt themselves to be children or offspring of the gods, to whom they owed their life and that of the earth and its many creatures. They would never have been tempted to take more from nature than they really needed. They felt a deep sense of culpability when they killed animals, felled trees or injured the earth. To be able to do this, nevertheless, they practised various rites in which they gained the gracious assent of the gods and of the high beings of the animals and plants that they used. The spiritual bond uniting them with the beings of nature that made their life on earth possible, was as yet a real experience for them.

Nowadays we live in an age when we need to try to re-establish this bond. Neither magic in the old sense nor mere imitation of traditional rituals are necessary for this. Rather, each person bears responsibility for strengthening their relationship with the earth and its creatures and entities, and for living their lives accordingly. Knowledge of the old rituals can help us to determine how we use our own powers and capacities, but is not essential for this. Every person can learn to rely upon themselves, to find their own connection, methods and approaches for serving the earth and supporting her creatures.

In the past a great responsibility lay with those who mediated communication with the gods. This gave them the authority to lead their tribes or peoples. Today there is no longer any reason for one person to exercise power over another. But this also has an effect on each person's individual responsibility. Each of us can feel how responsibility for the earth's well-being, for her life forces and condition, increasingly lies in our own hands.

*

The situation described above cannot be separated from another major human task in the modern age—dissolving and transforming existing ways in which power is wielded. Power structures are often a social poison, with a devastating impact on human beings and their ways of life. More than ever, individuals are seeking their personal freedom and scope for development. A free person, as becomes very apparent, suffers unspeakably in a society determined and governed in authoritarian ways. Power wielded over individuals who begin to feel and comprehend their intrinsic, essential being, elicits a pain in them that they can scarcely protect themselves from. We may regard such pain as unavoidable, and accept it. It could however be avoided if a shared view arose of the necessary preconditions for free human development. Power structures and authoritarian modes of governance are an attack upon the individual, shrouding and inhibiting our path toward our own most intrinsic being.

*

As human beings we also have duties toward the being of the earth. There is really no difference between those we have toward ourselves and those we have toward the earth.

What I do to transform myself I always also do for the being of the earth. Poet Nelly Sachs had deep experiences of the affinity between these two gestures. During her lifetime she wrestled with and for herself, for her own destiny and the earth's destiny. To her it was apparent that these two gestures are very painfully united. As a refugee from Germany who found safety in Sweden, she felt the sufferings of others as her own. Her poems give clear utterance to this. She writes in a letter to Johannes Edfelt:

> The whole of my life's work draws from this source: that during the 7 years under Hitler a person most beloved to me died as a martyr, and yet I did not lose my belief in our mission on earth: to pervade this dust with our pain, to illumine it; [and] that what we have accomplished in the dark, whether good or evil, will be inscribed in an invisible universe. What do we know? All of us wander in mysteries. [Dinesen/ Muesser, p. 209]

There is so much in these sentences that one falls silent. But in them can be felt a future which lies very close despite— or precisely because of—all suffering.

*

An essential question concerns the picture we have of the earth. That we relate to her as we do at present shows how mistaken this picture must be. We have distanced ourselves so far from the earth's reality that we no longer feel the pain we inflict upon her. We, her children, walk roughshod over our mother. We should not be surprised at the worries and problems that today weigh upon every single person and humanity as a whole, and can lead us to despair. From a higher perspective it is even necessary for those who treat the earth in this way to suffer. Our problems are of our own making and are due to fundamental misapprehensions. They arise when we lose sight of an original unity and ignore it.

Here we arrive at an important point in our reflections. Although we suffer because we are wounded and wound in turn, and are both victims and perpetrators, we find it difficult to perceive the causes of our suffering. Our irresponsible acts turn against the being of the earth, thus she to whom we owe our lives. We see no connection between our sufferings and our deeds. We do not even notice what we inflict on the earth through our deeds or misdeeds, for if we did we would comprehend such connections. We would behold the consequences of our actions, or at least feel them. And we would also perceive the degree to which they lead to the small personal misfortunes or catastrophes familiar to all of us.

We are blind in a way. It is hard for us to grasp that in life every act is always also a cause that has consequences for the whole. This whole, though, is the earth, or we can say the organism of the earth.

Now the being of our inner child, with whom this study is concerned, knows this. As a being of wisdom she knows about the living connections between separate entities, as well as the consequences every act has for the whole. Through our inner child, each of us participates in this wisdom and can connect with it. We can allow it to guide us, can feel our child, question her and ask counsel from her. We will now try to do exactly that.

2

Individuality and the inner child

After some important detours, we will now take up the thread again and address the inner child. In beholding her we notice her vulnerability. Her being has no defences against whatever affects her—she absorbs everything that happens. This also means that she takes upon herself what the individual suffers: taunts, insults, betrayal, blows, abuse. She absorbs everything bad, including bad things from past lives. It is her task to be receptive to whatever we repudiate, what we do not wish to acknowledge because we cannot endure it—what we cannot yet accept as a part of our being because it hurts too much. She absorbs all this so that it is not lost to us. She knows that we must not lose any of it since we would then be overlooking an essential part of ourselves. We would be standing on very shaky ground if we did not fully integrate, incorporate, what we have suffered and still suffer. The inner child knows that pain is as important as happiness if we are to develop and mature.

*

When we feel our way into the being of the inner child we notice that she does not only carry our pain. That is only one aspect of her mission. She breathes. She breathes in breadths that easily escape our rational mind. The inner child is a being who can lift herself far into realms of cosmic life. She has wings. To come to know her fully it is best to let her show us her wings. By this means we learn why she was created—not just to bear our pain but to carry us, our whole and perfect being. In fact, that is her primary task. She carries what we cannot yet carry ourselves. This is our pain but also our sacred, sublime being which, in our awareness, does not yet seem bound up with our earthly life. In our conscious mind we grasp only a certain aspect of our being, that which unites us with life on earth. The aspect of our being that unites us with higher worlds, with cosmic existence, escapes our attention. But we are also that. For the inner child it is an unquestionable fact that we reach far into cosmic worlds. This is precisely why she appears to us as a child—because our full and perfect being appears to our earthly consciousness in the guise of an innocent, childlike nature.

*

Encounters with the nature of the inner child are encounters with the cosmic being which every person also always is. With our inviolable being. She stands between the worlds as we do. But she does not call herself in doubt as we tend to. She does not despair or bind herself to things that contradict her inner nature. Meeting her is therefore a blessing for us since we easily despair at ourselves. The inner child tells us that we should never go so far as to sacrifice our child nature to the tasks we have taken on or been required to do. It is not worth it, for then we deny ourselves the powers which only we ourselves can draw upon, those wellsprings that lie in our cosmic nature.

*

To take seriously the messages which this being brings the person who listens out for her, shows us that we possess an intrinsic, irrepressible and untamed strength. The inner child is a teacher of our wildness. To the person who surrenders to her she speaks of strength and the longing for independence and freedom as an essential foundation of the human being. But we only do justice to this if we consciously experience within us the strength that endows us with autonomy and freedom. It is an important step in personal development to discover this strength within us, to live out of it, and to accept our destiny. The person who finds and accepts their wild nature only then truly stands up for themselves. What happens to them is no longer of no matter to them. They find their reason for living in sensing and hearkening to the living impulses they wish to follow, perceiving and accepting them, and turning them into reality. They experience the strength of self-determination as part of the nature of their own being.

*

Yet this wild nature has its shadow. This appears when someone does not have the courage to pursue their own life's impulses. Feeling your wildness, the strength of self-determination within you, does not yet mean that you live accordingly. There are consequences of surrendering to your own intrinsic nature, trusting and following it. You will inevitably meet obstacles. Today, when many people start to feel their own, intrinsic, individual strength and nature, it is a fundamental question as to how we learn to handle this untamed, freedom-seeking being. Experiencing our own individuality is only the first step; the next involves taking a stance and consistently following it even against the resistance which it calls forth. The inner child is a being who wishes to have a say in this important question of the modern age. To listen to her can help us find ways and strategies that do not overtax us yet still allow us to retain our dignity.

*

Every person is an intrinsic, original being and completely unique. To experience this uniqueness means pursuing a distinctive path. Of course we are already pursuing it, for every person has their own past in the form of many previous lives on earth. Today, however, it is possible to develop a clearer awareness of this path. We are learning to know this unique being of ours ever better. Each of us is strong, uncivilized, wild, uncomfortable and fiery, has wishes and many good ideas. We are unmannerly, obstreperous and full of devotion and love. We are very impatient, but also know how to wait. We want to have our wishes, ideas and concerns made reality. At the same time we are also vulnerable, sensitive and easily alarmed. The human individuality has many faces, many aspects, many colours. To accept our own being we need courage. We still have a way to go in practising this courage but should not despair if we have to keep starting all over again.

*

As we approach the wellspring our own self or, better, our own individuality, we arrive at a point where a curious and painful experience surfaces. We gain a conscious awareness of the strength we direct against ourselves. We perceive the numerous methods we resort to, to weaken and obstruct ourselves from becoming the person we have the potential to be. We discover how much we negate ourselves. This is a fundamental experience. We behold the resistance that lies within us and prevents us accepting the great, deep being we are. This point is a threshold at which many people stand today. They feel themselves as a being whose unfolding and furtherance they themselves prevent. They experience themselves standing in their own shadow.

But this is where we can become very active. We perceive the untrue judgements we make about ourselves and the lies we spread about ourselves. We perceive all that is mistaken in what we say and think about ourselves. We say that we are anxious, shy, greedy, that we are often angry, that our actions are unjust and egoistic. Each of us assigns a series of bad qualities to ourselves. There is some truth in this but also always some untruth since such characteristics fix, determine and manifest something that ought not to be fixed, determined and made manifest. These judgements arise from our ever-changing personality but not our whole being; the latter is different: broad, indeterminate, mobile and changeable. If we pay heed to it, address it, entrust ourselves to it and invoke it, our negative judgements also change. They lose their implacability and rigidity, become gentler and more alive. Then a point comes when we experience them more as guests, as entities inhabiting the soul which will, however, be glad to change and transform themselves. They do not wish to remain as they are. They bear false names which they would be glad to dispense with if we give them the opportunity. They are characterized by the fact that they do not wish to remain as they initially appear. They will gladly entrust themselves to the hands of the individuality who will accord them their true identity.

3
The wounds of the soul

One person whose destiny it was to experience the world's shadows intensely, at first hand, was Kaspar Hauser. In the spring of 1828 he appeared in Nuremberg, rocking unsteadily and unable to speak. During his lifetime there was already much speculation about him. In his childhood he had been intentionally kept in conditions intended to prevent him developing beyond the stage of an infant. After his release he surprised people around him with his astonishing abilities. At the age of 21 he fell victim to assassination. During his short life he suffered many torments. He was accused of being a swindler but also called 'The Child of Europe'.

Those who took his part noticed his unusual gifts. One of these was Friedrich Daumer, who wrote several books about him. Here is a longer quote from a report he wrote six months after Kaspar appeared:

> All his senses are of great sharpness and subtlety. For example, he smells things that have no smell at all for ordinary nostrils, from a considerable distance: tastes the smallest drop of meat stock that has fallen in his thin vegetable soup, and, from a distance of about one hundred paces can distinguish the separate berries of the bunches on an elder tree. At more than half this distance he discerns the difference between an elderberry and whortleberry. His eye, accustomed to the dark, can see fairly well still in an obscurity in which ordinary eyesight can perceive neither colours nor outlines. In what is for others complete darkness he can distinguish between dark brown, dark red, dark

green, black and suchlike; and at night he needs no light to find his way around the house, to go hither and thither quite safely. In fact he sees better in twilight than in the daytime, since daylight blinds him. Most remarkable are phenomena apparent in him that extend into the realm of animal magnetism and clairvoyance. In the night his illness broke, he had a dream in which his forthcoming recovery presented itself to him in a friendly picture. If someone approaches him unseen or unheard from behind, he knows this through a very unusual and unique sense that is awoken in him by the proximity of living beings. If one raises a hand to him he feels a disturbance issue from it which he designates by the expression 'being blown upon'. If he takes someone's hand, with only a few exceptions (with elderly persons), he feels a cold shiver. He displays most sensitivity to such impressions (for unknown reasons) in relationship to myself. With his back turned he feels it when I extend my hand toward him at a distance of one hundred and fifty paces. He shows a similar sensitivity toward metals: through the strength of attraction he distinguishes different metals which one hides beneath paper without him seeing or knowing. However these phenomena are diminishing, while at the same time he is now growing stronger and healthier. [Daumer, p. 24f.]

Reading these lines, one has to ask who this was who washed up on the shores of world history as Kaspar Hauser. He seems to have been destined to shine a special light upon the nature of the inner child. Kaspar Hauser suffered endlessly, falling into the hands of people who used him badly. His life story is archetypal in showing that we cannot avoid the aspects of life that are turned away from light. They arrive unasked and belong to us, as does guilt-less suffering. We do not yet have to understand why this is so, for we feel our capacities are as yet inadequate to do so. But we have embarked on the path of finding meaning in something that appears to have no rhyme or reason. It is no accident but part of our destiny that we also live in and with the darkness.

*

Yes, the gods have songs of which we know nothing more than, at most, the first few bars. They hum. Our ears are not yet accustomed to hear the Other, the inaudible that comes from them. We have settled upon judging the world according to its sensory raiment, but in doing so our hear-ing has grown weak. The gods have withdrawn from us, but only in order to return in a different guise: that is, in the guise of the human being who does not shy away from beholding the shadows and wounds in her own soul. This is why they supposedly disappeared: they withdrew so that we might learn to overcome the fear of our wounds and shadows and pain. But we will only manage this if we meet them with the strength of our inviolable being. We had to learn to dispense with the presence of the gods so that our inviolable, eternal being could dawn upon us.

The gods can scarcely understand our aversion to our wounds and hurts. For them, these are eyes. Our wounds are eyes through which the gods can perceive us. We have not yet learned that we perceive the world of the gods through them. The pain that humanity had to experience during the twentieth century is an unmistakeable picture and sign of this. The pain our wounds cause us should not deceive us. Fundamentally, this is the sign that we do not yet have the maturity to endure the world of the gods. As yet we are too impure, too unvirginal for the power of the gods not to hurt us. Really we are as yet far too unindividual. Our inviolable being is still in its labour pangs.

In the face of the wounds which our destiny inflicts upon us, we do not yet possess the strength to remain steadfast and to comprehend their meaning. We do not sufficiently experience the workings of the divine that speaks through our destiny, and this is why it must inflict pain upon us. We are still seeking the powers of soul that will enable us to intervene in our destiny before it injures us.

The wounds we feel are always also inflicted on us by the gods. They allow what is done to us to happen. What hurts is lack of meaning. If we understood our destiny before the gods needed to wound us, we would suffer far less. Then we could act in good time. As yet we rarely anticipate the gods, for we are still learning their language. It is very hard work for us to discover the meaning living in our destiny. Pain still always manages to take us by surprise. To pre-empt it is a goal we strive for. As yet we are still blinded by the light that shines from the gods; as yet their strength, their will, still paralyses us. But slowly things are improving: it is becoming easier for us to reflect upon ourselves and our divine nature.

*

The wounds of our inner child are numerous. We bear them with us like stigmata. They are inscribed in us and still hurt. They irritate us, appear burdensome and unnecessary. We want to rid ourselves of them. But that is a desire that will not be fulfilled. If we behold them without taking fright or being ashamed of them, it can seem that they are calling to us. The pain that issues from them is a kind of speech we must still learn. They are not meaningless. The very fact that they are unpleasant and that we hide them and try to unwish them, shows that they are central to us, key to us. Is it not so that they remind us of tasks to which we have not yet sufficiently addressed ourselves? We should learn from them.

Many of our inner wounds originate from past lives. In our wounds the wounds live on which we suffered, but also those we caused. We are beings who suffered but who also caused suffering. We are victims but also perpetrators. Both are wounds that repeatedly reappear through our destiny.

*

Those who succeed in looking at their own wounds without prejudice discover to their surprise that these appear to them as entities, beings. Naturally they disguise themselves: their clothes are outlandish and dark, repulsive, and this misleads us into overlooking their essential nature. But to patient observation, it becomes apparent that the negative image they present is only a guise. They deceive us. How could they do anything else, since they have arisen from denial, abasement and violence?

The role they play prevents us from living our full personality and individuality. They stand in the soul like walls we cannot get past. The power they have over us is indeed strange, and only the unredeemed form of their existence manifests in it. It is up to us to see that their dress of pain is not their true existence. At root they are not against us. Even if the pain they cause appears to rob us of our dignity, to shame us and to bring us to the limits of our endurance, they are far more than that. But they bear their secret deep within, and this secret is always also our own. In the powerlessness, fear and anxieties they cause they reveal to us only our own limits.

*

But this is not all. They always also show us how we can overcome and step beyond the limits that become visible through them. But for this we must regard them differently. Aversion and fear will not help us to understand their true nature, their real messages. It takes courage to regard them without judgement. To allow them power over us means chaining ourselves to a false picture. Our gaze is held by what they trigger in us, not by the intrinsic nature and being of the wounds themselves. They are not shame, fear, guilt. If we think this, we succumb to their appearance only.

The only way we can engage with them is by penetrating their seeming nature. To do this we adopt a stance toward them in meditation that is as far as possible without preconception. We show them that we want nothing from them. We simply behold them. With time, their willingness to reveal their true being becomes manifest. They have no desire at all to deceive us. They deceive us so that we can gain certain experiences through which we can grow and mature. But they are not what they accomplish in us in this way. They are more: they are greater, broader than the pain they cause.

4
Gestures of reconciliation

If the true being of our wounds is not manifest in the way they superficially appear, what then are their messages to us? They hide something from us. As we turn to them meditatively and as impartially as possible, we can feel a light shining within them, though one that remains vague and shadowy. It is as if this light is reaching our awareness from the future. A hidden, future quality of our being is actually shining through our wounds. The humiliation, shame and pain are heralds of a different time when we will have transformed ourselves. We are not there yet but our wounds will one day be healed. We will have grown and matured to the point when they no longer hurt us. And already they bear within them something of our future being.

Under every wound lies always also the strength to heal it. Here the secret work of the gods is revealed. They ensure a sacred balance in everything. In every wound lie pointers to what will heal it, signs of the activity and efficacy of our wise, higher being. In fact this being is already working upon us, but only in future will it become a part of our individual human nature. The gods cannot yet lead us on paths that are not obscure and dark. We have not yet come far enough. We still have much to learn. The blossoms of our high being are already there as seedlings and buds but as yet they still hurt.

This does not mean that we only develop through pain. The path of pain is one of many. There are also gentler, brighter, less arduous paths. But the dark paths often lead the way to brighter ones.

*

Behind a craving of some kind that we suffer from, because we repeatedly fall prey to it, lies a being apparent to attentive and non-judgemental discernment: a being that in no way resembles craving. A being appears that can be seen as the complementary picture to craving: a wise but also childlike being. For whatever reason, insufficient attention has been paid to it. It has been ignored and suppressed, and leads only a very impoverished existence. It comes to life again as a craving, like an evil caricature of its original nature. The reason we suffer from cravings does not lie in themselves. They point to something else, to a source that does however shine through them.

The key to freeing ourselves from a craving, therefore, does not lie within itself but in the being through whom it can reintegrate itself into the whole from which it has lapsed. In our present life, or in our previous life, it was unable to develop sufficiently. It was humiliated, abused, mistreated. To perceive its true nature, to affirm it, to build upon its existence and capacities, to accept these and to develop them, takes from a craving the strength and fire that keep it alive.

Other wounds, such as a sense of one's own inferiority, or humiliating people close to us or those we love, or betrayals, mistrust, philandering, disapproval and envy, likewise point to aspects of one's own personality and individuality that are undeveloped and have been suppressed, but which carry within them the longing to be discovered, accepted and developed.

All forms of fear, too, the tendency to flare up in fury, or the desire to be destructive, point to suppressed inner beings and aspects of our being.

It is quite likely that wounds and injuries of this kind will only be healed slowly. Time is needed. Often we have to reluctantly acknowledge that we are not in control of the length of time needed to heal wounds. They have their own rhythms and laws. But we will always find that as wounds heal, powers grow which benefit ourselves, certainly, but also those around us.

*

And now we can ask what we actually are above and beyond our flaws, wounds and also our abilities and successes. To my astonishment I do not find myself in whatever I have failed in and made a mess of, nor in whatever I have achieved. I am not the one who failed nor the one who was successful. What I can't do is not me, nor am I what I can do. I feel myself forbidden from regarding myself as the one who was rejected or the one who was praised. In the light I experience as my own, as my inmost and most valuable possession, neither subsist. I cannot believe that I appear to myself only through my successes or failures. The one I am deep within stands above and beyond either. But where?

This question relates to a further experience, the pain of grasping that we cannot yet form any picture of ourselves at all. We cannot know who we are because we have not yet reached the place where we could become apparent in our entirety. Our own perception fails before the being we will one day become. And the pictures we have of ourselves, those we have previously formed, are not true, for they are only partly true. How can we know how much they show us of ourselves, or how much they do not yet show?

We might say we are gods who do not possess themselves at all, gods on the way to becoming. We grow only slowly, very slowly, toward ourselves. I do not and I cannot yet possess myself. I am beyond the reach of all images I can make of myself. What I know of myself so far is only a trace, a light-trail of my true being. I am still foreign to myself because I do not yet have the capacity to perceive my whole being. Thus a veil lies before my inner gaze. I am still in the process of growing beyond me toward myself. I am and am not what I discern of myself. I already say 'I' to myself but it is not *the* I. I know very well indeed that I cannot force a knowledge of what I do not yet know of myself. To do this would only make me miserable. But this does not mean doing nothing. My wounds make sure that I stay awake.

*

The inner child watches over the blind god who is hidden from himself. Nevertheless he stands upright, albeit unsteadily, and follows his paths, though hesitantly and doubtfully. Somehow he manages it. The human I, after all, is not left to its own devices. Things would go badly if this were so. The human I is not a being thrown back entirely on its own resources. Care is given it, it is taken care of, day after day, night after night. It is integrated into the great cycles of cosmic life. Growing and dying, day and night, waking and sleeping, death and life: these accompany its existence and shape it. The I becomes itself through the rhythms which hold sway over the earth. We should not forget this. The earth and nature, both cosmic and terrestrial, are mother and father of the human I, and it could not exist without them. Its life still largely relies upon them. The sphere which it calls its own is still small in scope.

5
The secret of darkness

When we go inward we not only meet woundedness but also evil. Fearful, terrifying gods also live within us. Their grimaces alarm us, rob us of reason and self-control. They not only teach us fear but we deny their existence too. They are so evil that we cannot endure the sight of them. We do not dare to speak of them since we think that even uttering their names would encourage them to surface in us. We therefore tend to suppress their existence. But they are there and cannot be ignored. Hatred, envy, revenge are the names of some of them. To be inhabited by these spirits of destruction and annihilation, to be their life and dwelling place, brings endless shame.

We know we deceive ourselves when we think we can rid ourselves of them by denying them. They are great, strong gods and cannot be overlooked. They deserve a different treatment. As we can intuit, they have their purpose. If it is our task to raise ourselves from blind to seeing gods, it is only right that they too, the evil gods, should have the right to inhabit us. We, and they too, must not be excluded from anything, but all must find its right and proper place.

*

'We are perfect because of our imperfections', cries Kae Tempest in her great poem 'Brand New Ancients'. Later she offers a striking characterization of the blind gods:

> The gods are on the beach holding hands beneath
>   the stars
> The gods are on the street washing their cars

the gods are visiting their parents, they're talking
    'bout the past
helping their new nieces make papier-mâché masks
for the school play, the gods can't wait to have a lie in,
the gods are getting on with it, the gods are really
    trying.
The gods are throwing dirt on the coffin of a loved one,
blaming themselves, wondering what they done wrong;
the gods are in the kitchen making dinner for their
    mates,
but now they've had a row and now they've
    smashed a couple of plates,
the gods are up early again, working late,
standing in a queue feeling sick, got the shakes,
the gods have had enough, they got nothing left to hate,
but they like to watch the sun when it settles on the
    lake,
the gods are on their knees feeling lost and exhausted,
deadlines, debts, divorces,
forgotten our calling,
forgotten our wisdom,
forgotten how to speak to ourselves, how to listen.
But the gods are in the theatres, the gods are playing
    strings,
the gods are staring at the trees as they move in the wind,
the gods are right here, as far-fetched as it sounds:
everyone's a god, no kings, no crowns,
just us, one being, infinite and holy,
gods, messed up, lonely,
squashed, stressed out, dumbed down, raging,
wasted … Same as it ever was: brand new ancients.*

The human being possesses all aspects of existence. We
are a distinctive mix of light and shadows. We bring forth

*Kae Tempest, from *Brand New Ancients*, Picador 2013.

colours that can only appear through us. To be able to be imperfect is both curse and grace. Yes, we can go astray and go haywire, we can fall, deceive and be deceived, most easily about ourselves. But that is who we are. That is how we are. That is our frailty and our wonderful gift and offering.

*

To look evil in the eye and not grow angry is a great challenge to us today. Evil seeks to be seen. It no longer makes any efforts at all to disguise itself. It can do no other than reveal itself to all. Since the last century its destructive potency has become unmistakeably apparent, its desire for destruction. As if that's what it wanted: to be seen and absorbed by human awareness. The events of the last century make clear that evil is no longer skulking in the shadows, because it wants to be accepted, wants to be absorbed by humankind.

The secret of evil is that it cannot be destroyed. It is indestructible for it destroys. The desire to destroy it only lengthens its life since this does not transform it. To push it under means only that it surfaces somewhere else because it has not been changed. To accept it does not mean bringing ourselves down to its level but offering it the possibility of transformation.

*

The other secret of evil is that it transforms itself within and through the human being. Yes, we succumb to it but that is not all. Evil seeks us out because it can come to expression in us and act within us; but it also seeks us out because we ensure its redemption. Evil beholds in us a being within whom it can come to effect but one who at the same time embodies a promise: that we can walk onward into the light. For human beings this means staying upright even when everything else is bent and crooked, and preserving our truth despite all that is false, deceptive and mean around us. Yet how easily outer conditions gain sway over us. It can make us despair. How easily, despite all our best intentions, do we lose our capacity to stay true and upright. We think it ought to be easy.

The god we are has no simple path to follow. We are not relieved of the need to live, to work, to worry, to feel envy to seek meaningless distraction, to live in illusions and hopes. But that is not all. There is much more. We must not succumb to the darkness. Even if it takes time, even if many circuitous routes lead us through uncertain, twilight lands, through pain, loss, grief, fear, self-rejection and shame, we can be sure that precisely this is the path of our higher mission.

The gods who, unlike us, can never inhabit the earth, envy us the experiences we have here. Even the dark and terrifying gods do so, the ones we would most like to repulse. The gods would like to be where we are. They even envy us the experiences we have at the threshold of death. All we experience is always also for them, the high and sublime beings of the cosmos. This is why they never leave us and why we need never feel abandoned by them. The beings of cosmic existence look attentively at how we deal with evil, what stance we take to it, how we define our task in relation to it, and how we help heal it.

*

Where we lose ourselves to powers that turn against our I, the danger is greatest that we will be weakened. These powers live in us and test us. It seems grotesque that the more we reject and dismiss them, the stronger they become. They will not let themselves be dispelled by our efforts to diminish them even though they themselves diminish us through the great power they wield. Transforming them depends on how we meet them. They wish to engross us and weaken us. But nothing is gained by responding to them in a way that vilifies, denies or demonizes them, for then the vicious circle only begins all over again. Then we simply succumb to them still more.

But if we find the courage to hold the gaze of those entities or beings who embody evil, to stand up to them, then they show that they look up to us. Indeed they cast an envious eye upon someone who knows how to see through their grotesque masks, because such a person possesses the key to their transformation, and emanates the powers which heal evil. Such a person heals through their capacity to resist evil without condemning it.

*

Where evil is too much for our capacities to deal with it, where it is greater than we are, the powers of our I are not equal to it. We are at risk of succumbing to it because we are not strong enough to set limits to its scope. It overwhelms us. Then there is little point in fighting it. Alone, we will get no further. Then we need to look around for fellow combatants, for friends or those who can offer us advice and help. It will be essential for us to develop new soul powers. In the face of evil in the modern era, we all encounter the key and existential question of how we can practise and develop soul forces that will help us to resist both inner and outer evil. Where our powers fail in the face of evil, there is nothing else to be done but actively work to develop new powers of the soul.

To overtax ourselves in the encounter with evil is not wise. We need an exact and healthy estimation of our own powers. In this way we learn to know our own limits in the work of transforming evil. Then we do not succumb to the danger of exceeding them.

6
The wisdom of the body

Evil is the deepest wound. That is why it is so difficult, and repeatedly difficult, not to give up when faced with evil. Basically we have no choice but to keep accepting it again and again. But this work will only succeed if we cultivate patience and endurance. And it always starts where we accept ourselves—precisely at the place where we interrupt our continual self-criticizing and self-blame. We ourselves are the cause of this and it saps our strength. We always start to grow stronger where we make room for our longing to be reconciled with ourselves. But this means actively embarking on the path of self-transformation. We do not have to hide from ourselves. There is still so much we can discover in ourselves. We are the person we are and yet we are still only growing into this. To discern and develop our own abilities and gifts is something we are all beginners at.

Evil, absurdity, darkness urge us to become aware of our own powers and wellsprings. This is possible only if we comprehend and experience ourselves as beings who carry within them the seeds of their own development. We protect and safeguard what we are walking towards, working our way towards. The seeds of our future being, which is still slowly dawning, do not have to be created by us, for they have long existed. They are waiting for us to perceive them, to be acknowledged and to grow. This is why working on ourselves is more like a game of hide-and-seek than a strict, self-denying and arduous labour. The abilities we wish to acquire are already germinally present. Some have developed already, have proven their worth, while others still await their unfolding.

*

A key question arises here for every single person. It concerns our relationship with our own body. The well-springs of our soul forces serve to nurture our capacities for steadfastness and authenticity, but so too do the powers of our own body. The more we feel one with it, the easier it becomes to face reality, including its dark aspects, without losing too much of our strength. Identity with our own body is a powerful source which helps the soul to live in a self-determining and self-responsible way. The body bears me. I owe my earthly existence to it. I can work through it, can think, feel, perceive, love and so forth. Only with the body am I whole.

With some dismay we can discover how our long history has helped alienate us from the body. It has been seen as 'low', worthless, bad, wrong, uncontrolled, wild. We have learned to master it, to suppress it, to mistreat it and to exploit it. Today we are struggling to reach a healthy, balanced relationship with it. The development of the personality can only unfold with, and never against, the body. Its needs are essential. The body is a being we should not master and control but value if we wish to live at peace with it.

*

The body is a being like plants, trees and animals. It is an animate, ensouled and spirit-endowed entity. It speaks to the one it belongs to. It has something to tell us. It speaks through its conduct and states. Basically, our human destiny speaks through it. If we learn to hearken to it, we will find it easier to understand and unfold our own destiny.

In fact, attentiveness towards the body holds great potential for transforming the personality. The better we know it, its signs and states, the simpler it is to respond in a right and appropriate way to events in our own destiny. The body gives signs which are in harmony with what occurs outwardly, not at odds with it. The body is an extremely wise being and it is not a good idea to dispense with this wisdom or to fail to take its communications seriously.

We can read the body like a script, like a book. It is a partner on the paths of destiny. Basically it is impossible to act contrary to it. What it offers us it utters through us, but also expresses itself through obstacles, pain and illnesses. These are part of its symbolic language. To ignore them means to leave key pointers unused. The tiredness we feel in the evening has meaning, as does the pain the body causes us. It speaks through the illnesses it grants us, for they admonish us to attend to the need for transformation.

*

To respond to pain and illness by regarding them as the expression of a meaningful language that wants to draw our attention to something we should become more aware of, creates a fraternal relationship with our body. The more we live our way into the reality of the divine world, the more important does this relationship with our body become. The body does not become less but more important. This may seem surprising since you might think that finding your way into worlds of spirit is like an ascent that involves releasing yourself from the body's needs and compulsions. But that is not the whole truth. The path into the world of spirit, you see, is at the same time a descent, an ever-deepening connection with matter, not with its shadow but with its spiritual essence. The body is our material companion. Like the animals and plants it is a wise, spirit being that wishes to be perceived and valued as such.

The sense of unity that rises from our own body and encompasses the soul dispenses a fundamental stability which the human soul today so greatly needs. The soul can learn to trust in the body and the harmony that exists between both. The body is very trustworthy, especially when it announces itself. It does so on behalf of the person with whom it is connected, often in a higher sense that only becomes apparent gradually.

7

Conversations with our inner child

Conscious development of our personality must not be coupled with bitterness and self-denial. Despite everything, inner growth resembles a game—it resembles children's play that is fuelled by a pure joy in life and yet absolute seriousness. To develop ourselves is an act of liberation. Inner growth cannot be compelled. Rather: at last we may walk the path of transformation, in joy and pleasure and self-responsibility for the wellspring of our own being. If we develop a sense for the joy that is deeply inscribed in all transformation, we stand within the aura of our inner child. Then she stands up in the soul because she knows herself to be seen and valued and accorded dignity. If compulsion, excessive will or dogmatism get mixed up with this, strength is lost. The soul that is too earnest or bitter cannot find itself. It only discovers itself in play, that is, in lightness of being, of liveliness, interest. Imagination is required for this—no game develops without it. Whoever is transforming themselves is always a child, an artist.

Change happens easily above all. Anything over-tense, fixedly determined, rigid, will tend to harden the soul rather than broaden and open it. This does not mean that, when appropriate, we should not also be strict with ourselves, practise renunciation—but never without at the same time cultivating a loving care for ourselves. Development of the personality can only be meaningful when it is accompanied by a feeling of inner joy, of unconditional self-respect and self-acceptance.

*

By nature the human being is both perfect and imperfect. We are a divine being. We carry within the gifts of transforming and ennobling ourselves. We are right to assure ourselves of these gifts, to respect them. If we exert compulsion upon ourselves, if we punish ourselves, subject ourselves to strict and unfulfillable precepts, we run the danger of denying our perfect being. In doing so we internalize certain thought patterns, subordinating ourselves to them as we seek to realize them. But it is fundamentally and essentially wrong to subordinate ourselves. Instead, we should seek our own sources, which lie only within ourselves as the divine beings we are. We draw from these wellsprings. Yet they are not informed by particular models and precepts but only by the essential being of our individuality. To accept it, come to know it, to learn to act out of it, is a primary goal of our time.

*

Our wounds are always also our shadows, and our shadows are always also our wounds. When we do wrong we do so because there is something lacking in us. Where we fall short we become bad. Resentment, lack of respect, disdain, meanness, cruelty and destructive rage are not freely chosen conduct. They do not originate in the free individuality of the divine human being. Evil can only unfold its power when it finds a lack, a wound, a vulnerability. We can only become evil where we are not yet in balance, where we lapse from the unity of our being, where our wishes and needs are ignored or we ourselves ignore them. True harmony of soul renders evil impossible. The developed human individuality stands in unity with itself, affirms its whole, complete being which forbids it to surrender to evil.

*

The being of our inner child seeks to reincorporate into the human individuality what has lapsed from unity with it. She can only do so thanks to her cosmic nature. The inviolable and invulnerable part of her cosmic being gives her the strength to do this. We can let her lead and guide us so that we come to discern the aspects of our being that have been excluded from integration into our nature. She points us to these aspects, to our hurts and wounds. But at the same time she points us to the powers of soul that enable us to be reconciled and reunited with soul aspects that have become estranged from us, that have been repudiated. The inner child endows us with the powers of awareness necessary to accomplish the work of healing upon our own soul, our own being. She gives us a certainty of our own inviolability. She strengthens us to become aware of the presence of our own cosmic being. She wants to help us find the capacity to become at home in ourselves.

*

We were speaking of Kaspar Hauser. We beheld his highly sensitive nature. Now let us turn to a further aspect of his being, once more expressed in the words of Friedrich Daumer:

> When Hauser emerged from concealment and entered the world, his soul was the mirror and reflection of a heavenly goodness, purity and innocence, unlike anything hitherto known or appearing. These qualities

did not remain. But it is a fact that they were present, that these most rare and remarkable of all moral phenomena did actually appear observably among us. Apart from the testimonies of my own relations, others of the most demonstrable and concordant kind confirm it. Indeed, it can be proven that though Hauser fell into a certain volatility during the further course of his life in the world, he remained such a good, noble and lovable human being to his very last breath that humanity would be assured of happiness if all or even a majority of people resembled this picture. It was not only the romantic rarity of his fate and his appearance that drew and captivated people, but the whole unique childlike and loving qualities of his being and unblemished beauty of his soul that exerted such a wonderful magic. [...] He felt every pain and every misfortune that happened to others, or even only seemed to happen, as his very own. He could not be induced to strike another person even in jest; this, he said, hurt him too much. The cold, cold-hearted isolation of human selfhood and cautiousness, this true Fall of Man, had not yet appeared in him. In his moral being and constitution one could behold here an archetype of paradisal humanity, a miracle worthy of reverence within a wholly ruined human world plunged in its abyss of self-seeking and malice. [Karl Heyer, p. 76ff.]

Karl Heyer also quotes Baron von Tucher, who came to a similar conclusion about the intrinsic nature of Kaspar Hauser:

As I experienced and described this human being, with his natural purity and lack of self-consciousness, he presented to the most perfect degree a picture of the first man in Paradise before the Fall. [p. 79]

Once again it is apparent that a preoccupation with the being of Kaspar Hauser is fruitful for our enquiries. Turning to him, we can gain a greater sense of the connection between the nature of the wounded and the cosmic child. It seems as if his destiny is an important sign that can help us see human nature in a new and different light. Through him we can learn something about human nature that will only dawn fully in future, but already appeared with him. His fate is part of a symbolic language through which the being of the inner child, together with her cosmic nature, has inscribed itself in human consciousness.

*

It is possible to hold conversations with our inner child. The task of the inner child is to serve a person's destiny. The more consciously we work with her, the easier it becomes for us to fulfil our mission. To do this we need to practise a listening that surrenders itself entirely to another being. The inner child is a spiritual being who reveals herself only to our inner senses. If we behold her, we do so in our inner eye. We can feel her being, her closeness, her attentiveness and support. We can awaken to the healing impulses that issue from her. But to do this we cannot rely on our outer senses, only on our inner, spiritual ones. This means that we must develop special trust in our inward experiences. This trust grows with practice, through repeated and patient attention to the being of our inner child.

*

The inner child is willing to consider our questions and also anxieties, and to give us counsel. But she depends on us giving her room to make her appearance. This room is a soul space without judgement, fixed ideas and expectations, and is needed so that the inner child can enter into conscious conversation with us.

If we succeed in creating inner tranquillity, composure and freedom from preconceptions, we will be able to sense the being of the inner child. She will announce herself. She will show herself and speak, and respond to questions. We will be able to observe her and become aware of the work she accomplishes for and through us. The inner child works upon us, spiritually giving us gifts that help to enliven, strengthen and heal us.

8
The nature of the cosmic child

Conscious encounter with the inner child is an occurrence of great significance. Those who seek her enter into a connection which begins to free them from the lies that they have built up about themselves. They can no longer deceive themselves. They can behold themselves through the gaze of the inner child. Nothing remains hidden from this gaze. We see ourselves as we are, without masks. Equally we learn no longer to be ashamed of ourselves, for the gaze of the inner child is without any accusation or blame.

We feel within us a wariness of great-sounding words. We become humble. Also quieter. We feel that something stands guard over the words we speak. We do not tolerate arrogance, hasty judgements, or lies, however little they be. But our relationship to our own actions changes too. They must not do harm. They must not cause unhappiness to anyone else.

Let us acknowledge that this is not always a condition that is easy to endure. To be a child as an adult is not something we are accustomed to. Backward steps are natural. On no account should we despair if we do not yet succeed in everything that we undertake. The child forgives. She does not want us to apply a false pressure to ourselves, nor be too strict or too sharp with ourselves. She does not tolerate the ambition through which we make an enemy of ourselves. She wants us to experience happiness, joy at what is already going well.

*

We never finish learning from the inner child. She teaches the soul throughout its whole life, in fact really throughout its many earthly lives. Her messages are therefore diverse and individual, directed to the individual human being. Each person hears the teachings of the inner child in their own way. Nevertheless I would like briefly to summon here the mood in which the inner child can reveal herself to each of us. These seven phrases can help you to be more open to the particular messages you receive. They are part of a schooling that I received:

— Human being, imbue your wounds with your own intrinsic, sacred I substance.
— Behold the beings that your wounds originally are.
— Stand in your intrinsic, personal light.
— In the breath of your soul that leads you through day and night, through the year and through death into a new life, the true healing powers for your being are revealed.
— Behold and acknowledge the helping powers that reveal themselves in the outer world, in animals, plants, landscapes, cultures and in the course of ages.
— Accept that you are accepted.
— And accept yourself, life, destiny and peace.

*

In Chapter 2 of this section we said that the inner child breathes, that she can raise herself on her wings into the realms of cosmic life. The inner child has many faces: as pioneer of human individuality the cosmic worlds are anything other than foreign to her. We can see the cosmic aspect of her being as the highest expression of the inner but also the wounded child. Her power of devotion allows her to live in all worlds, making her an indispensable and precious companion to human individuality. The being of the inner child is not identical with the human I, but she receives it, enfolds it and accompanies it through all the lives that it leads on earth.

The cosmic child is the aspect of the inner child that serves the sacred individuality of the human being by opening it to the breadths of cosmic existence. The rhythmic breathing inherent in the cosmic child unites us with the wisdom of the divine world, enabling the soul to feel itself as a being whose birthplace is not only on earth but also in the divine world. The human being is a child of the cosmos and the earth. Within us two streams of life and existence unite.

The wings of the cosmic child unite the human I with the divine world. Inscribed in them are the treasures of wisdom which we can attain when we raise ourselves consciously into the divine world. As we behold the wings of the cosmic child, we become aware of the treasures of wisdom that become available to us when we grow conscious of our cosmic nature.

*

The divine world is manifold. Earthly human beings will only slowly be able to open themselves to this world. Only the noblest and highest powers of our soul are able to lend us the strength that we need in order to retain our conscious awareness when we meet the divine world. To read the script of the wings of the cosmic child is therefore not an undertaking to which we can apply ambition or over-determined enquiry. Rather, we need reverence, humility but also rigour towards ourselves.

The wings of the child caress the whole cosmos. They spread far abroad into the high secrets of existence. To feel the strength and grandeur of these wings strengthens and expands our own soul. Thereby we feel elevated and invigorated. We feel our own wings growing if we turn towards those of our cosmic child and entrust ourselves to them.

The wings of the cosmic child penetrate the worlds which the soul enters after death, and from which it departed before its birth on earth. The cosmic child is united with the divine beings who have accompanied human beings since primordial times. It is easy and joyful for her to connect with the ancient gods, with Horus, Athene, Thor and all the others. She also stands close to the gods of indigenous tribes, as well as to divine entities who inspire humanity's great religions. It is striking to perceive the immediacy and unconstrained freedom with which the cosmic child meets sometimes conflicting religious traditions. We can feel her impulse to turn to all of them with respect and empathy.

*

Intrinsic to the being of the cosmic child is the gesture of expansion and broadening. Her powers of devotion turn to the higher worlds, to worlds of spirit, their beings and powers. This is why she can also turn to each person's higher being, which has not yet united with the earthly world. The cosmic child trusts in the whole human being, her devotion is sufficient to behold and receive our higher being. She teaches us to accept our whole and perfect nature. With the power of devotion she affirms our whole being. The cosmic child serves the human being's individuality in so far as she prepares us to receive our higher nature.

She has the task of uniting the various aspects of the human individuality so that they can live in harmonious interplay. The cosmic child forms a unity with the inner child and therefore does not run the risk of connecting with the world of spirit in a one-sided way. The spiritual nature of the human being must not develop at the cost of earthly destiny but must be able to serve this. The transformation of destiny, healing of the forces of evil and redemption of the earth remain the primary goal of the inner child, of the cosmic aspect of her being, and of the human individuality.

This is why the cosmic child maintains a deep relationship with the earth. However, her attention is not focused on the earth's material aspects but on its aspects of soul and spirit. The cosmic child unites the human soul with the living cosmos but also with the hidden spirit form of the inner earth.

The cosmic child spurs the human individuality to surrender to the profound secrets of the earth. It is her task to show us that the earth possesses healing forces. The cosmic child shows the human soul paths that lead into the mysterious realm of the earth's interior, to discover there how our true and healing life impulses are deeply united with the being of the sacred earth. The cosmic child wants to show the human soul that its task involves standing between the heavenly realms and the sacred realms of the inner earth. The healing efficacy and activity of the human soul consists of the uniting of these two realms within itself.

*

The inner child and the aspects of her being are concerned with the transformation of pain but also with the transformation of the shadow and evil. This is true too of the cosmic child.

Her wide breath, the spread and motion of her coloured and luminous wings, stand precisely for the gesture and the vigour of union and healing. The cosmic child embodies the order of being that seeks to mend all division, not by avoiding transformation but by promoting it. True transformation does not avoid pain. Those who acknowledge pain, who do not withdraw from the mysteries of the earth and of their own being, nor fall into consternation, are working in accord with the cosmic child. They do not shy away from the shadows. They can do this because they feel within them the strength of a confidence nourished by the active power of the cosmic child. The cosmic child leads the wounded and suffering soul upon her wings into the heavenly realms, but also into the sacred realms of the inner earth, to strengthen and invigorate it for the tasks and labours it must accomplish to fulfil its earthly goals.

9

Knowledge of human nature and the inner child

The being of the inner child has no end. Trying only to encompass her in thought swiftly meets its limits. This is due above all to the cosmic aspect of her being. The being of the inner child reveals herself to direct experience. She wishes to speak to the individual person. She is a speaking being. Her pure and virginal nature repudiates merely intellectual thinking, but is all the more apparent to inner perception.

Through her purity of being, the inner child stands in a special relationship with the ages. Within her the ages stand still, and past and future unite. This grants the soul room in which it can look in all directions in all tranquillity. This leads to deep insights. For those who seek this, the inner child can mediate a deep knowledge of the world and also of the human being. Admittedly, such knowledge of the human being as we so far possess is in its infancy, but it's a start.

*

Alongside the inner child, in whom are united the virginal-cosmic and the wounded nature of the human being, with all the intermediate stages between them, other beings also become apparent. Two of these beings are the feminine and masculine aspect of the individual person. These have been formed in our past lives by experiences in the broadest sense bound up with gender. Every human individuality has usually already experienced life as both man and woman. It has had many mothers and fathers, and has itself also experienced giving birth and procreating, has itself been both father and mother. It has been loved, and also hurt, by men and women, and has also loved and inflicted hurt as both man and woman. The relationship which the individuality forms with the genders arises from experiences it has gathered in this way. The masculine and feminine nature of the human being each have their own very particular and individual form, and are in each case distinct beings. If we wish, we can discern and experience these masculine and feminine aspects in us. We can perceive our man and woman, or rather our male and female natures, as independent beings dwelling within us. And we will be able to enter into conversation with these soul aspects, which are also beings of soul.

*

There are further aspects of the soul as well. Every person stands within earth's evolution, or we could also say within earth's karma, in their own way. We are always also a part of the great and dramatic process of the earth's evolution. We have lived during many epochs and undertaken various different tasks. Each of us has a particular stance toward the being of the earth, bound up with our individuality. This aspect of the soul, too, has the character of a distinctive being. The earth, her evolution, her travails, her needs, and the numerous beings connected with her, are bound up with each individual in a very particular way. These affect us, speak to us, invoke in us specific reflections and decisions. They impinge upon our inner nature, move us, instigate our actions and elicit particular intuitions within us. We belong to the earth in an immediate, inseparable way, are deeply bound up with her by virtue of our numerous experiences, and therefore experience and feel the earth in our own distinctive fashion. We are borne up and sustained, but also bear and sustain in turn. This being or entity we become aware of has a marked transpersonal aspect, but is also part of each person's individuality. Through it becomes manifest our earthly history which has led us through the epochs of earth's evolution.

*

We encounter a further aspect of our being when we contemplate our own personal path. There we behold ourselves, the experiences we have gathered through our numerous earthly lives. But besides these we also possess experiences in the world of spirit. The traces we have left behind on the earth go hand-in-hand with those in worlds of spirit. Besides our earthly biographies, we have biographies in supersensible worlds, to which we are only slowly awakening. The being referred to here encompasses both our earthly and cosmic experiences. All our incarnations, all our paths through life are united within it. Approaching this being, we can gain a living impression of our own I nature, our individuality.

*

These five beings—the inner child, the masculine and feminine being, the being who unites earth's evolution with our individuality, and our I-being or individuality itself—are joined by a sixth. This entity mediates between the human being and the being of the inner, hidden earth. The earth's interior becomes an ever more important experience for those who embark on the path of their spiritual development. Their development is anything other than independent of the deep nature of the earth. In fact our own path of evolution is existentially connected with it. The interior of the earth, her nature, her light, but also her shadows, has a deep connection with human evolution. The stages of our development are basically inherent in the earth's spiritual being, her spiritual organism. Our evolution only has meaning in connection with the existence of the earth's interior. This fact is embodied in the sixth aspect of our being.

On the one hand we share in the shadows of the earth's interior, and our evolution is decisively informed by them. The shadows which we must transform as individuals on our path of development are always also connected with the shadows the earth bears within herself. On the other hand, we are also united with the earth's light, with her pure, redeemed being. We always also live our individual earthly life out of this light.

The nature of the inner earth is significant for the individual in that it is an archetype of the powers we encounter as shadow and light within us and within our lives.

The earth as a being of spirit and soul is united with the human being, with every human individual. Human evolution is bound up with the earth, which reveals her depths and living nature only to those who can penetrate and behold her sacred depths. A person's development always also encompasses the shadow beings who live in the sacred halls of the earth's interior. We cannot avoid also attending to *their* development and evolution.

As human beings we stand within the shadows of the being of earth, but also within her light. Our evolution always also serves the earth's transformation. Within the earth's interior is a golden land which we can call Shambala, to which this sixth aspect of our being is beholden.

Its light shines into the human soul. We perceive this light when we experience how our soul's luminous nature seeks the luminosity of the earth's interior. A bright thread unites our soul with the light of the inner earth. This thread is an important and decisive measure of our own spiritual and other development. With it, we can find our way, for within it shines the light of our own path. It consists of particular stages or gateways that lead, instruct and support us on our individual path of transformation.

*

With a consideration of those aspects which constitute us, which form a unity with the being of the inner child, we reach a preliminary end to our investigations. Wherever the accounts given here initially seem inaccessible to conceptual or rational understanding, they open all the more to meditative contemplation and enlivening. But this is also the path of individualization of thoughts. Thinking longs to be nurtured and nourished. Meditation is the means for this. Thinking often lacks abundance and warmth. By experiencing thoughts in their depths, we ensure that they are warmed through once more.

III
SEVEN MEDITATIONS

The following seven meditations aim to help deepen under-standing of the being of the cosmic child, and give deeper individual access to some of the accounts in this book. It is best to engage with them in as free a way as possible. How we approach them can only emerge from the experiences we gain through our own contemplation.

Those who engage with these meditations will quickly notice that they militate against any merely intellectual approach. A solely conceptual preoccupation with them will fail. One does justice to them best of all by allowing them time to unfold slowly within the soul.

They leave traces in the soul to which we can begin to attend. They sink under then surface again, fade away and rise up anew. They develop a play and interplay in the soul. By becoming aware of this play, we awaken to the formative forces these meditations elicit in the soul.

Every meditation, and also every verse and every line, points the soul in a particular direction. This can be expe-rienced as a living echo of the meditation, verse or line. It is very beneficial to become aware of the inner resonances and reverberations of the words, for by doing so we can perceive the powers underlying them. A deeper, more attentive reading and hearkening begins.

It is a good idea to divide these paths into smaller stages; sometimes a line or a word is enough.

*

These meditations point to various dimensions of the cosmic child. The nature of the cosmic child has a close relationship with the human being and the earth. The living earth is the sustaining ground of the human being. She passes healing forces to us (meditation 1) and forms a unity with us (2). The heart impulses of human beings have great significance for the being of the earth (3). Likewise, our individual connection with our cosmic child affects the life and existence of the earth (4). As the divine beings we are, we are given special responsibility for the earth (5). Each of us can sharpen our perception of the fact that the world of spirit endows us with special and distinctive gifts (6). As divine beings we can try to attend and hearken to our inner voice (7).

*

There are noticeable connections between the meditations. Thus they can be arranged in a six-pointed star, with the seventh meditation at the centre. The meditations of each triangle form a unity together. The meditations of the standing triangle (verses 1, 3, 5) mediate aspects that point to our tasks in relation to the earth and its transformation. Attention is drawn to the tasks assigned to us as beings of the earth and the cosmos. The meditations of the other triangle (verses 2, 4, 6) follow a different soul gesture: they point to the soul capacity of devotion. We always also receive the gifts of the cosmos. By becoming conscious of these gifts and perceiving our cosmic being, we can also more easily fulfil our tasks on earth.

Between facing meditations (1-6, 2-5, 3-4) there are also connections or relationships that enhance the different qualities of each.

But these meditations also form a developmental sequence leading from the first to the seventh.

These pointers to the patterns and laws inherent in the meditations are cursory since they are intended only to stimulate your own discoveries.

Health
is the holy power
of the interior cosmos
of the soul

Acknowledging oneself
means
acknowledging the divine being
that every person is
as a being
of cosmic existence

Draw from the wellsprings of existence
in which your soul reposes
like a child
draw from the light
that the sun gives the earth
draw from the realms
of the living atmosphere
draw from the manifold waters
and draw from the halls of the sacred earth

Seek the beings in the elements
who surround
envelop
sustain
you
and you will receive
the health
of living existence

2

Earth you are so good
    you bear us
        protect us
            nourish us
                transform us

You are our inmost being
the loving embrace of our destiny
in you we live—we watch—we work

Our being is your being
What you give us
we give you again
by seeking our paths of destiny
                our powers of love
          our life resolves
       our steps of transformation

In the realms of your being
we find our whole being
The time will come
when we have found ourselves
in you
for already you shine
in the paths
we walk in peace
with ourselves and with existence

3

Earth
we love you
you bear us
from darkness into light
protect us
give us the peace
that is deep in us
which we bear
as the light of our heart
in order to bless
the work of our hands
and the meaning
that speaks from everything
from the being of cosmic harmonies
from the workings of cosmic spirits
to liberate
      to transform
            to redeem
the darkness
in the name of the all-present deity in us

Yes, earth
your spirits of life unite you
with the impulses of our hearts
so that existence grows
the spheres of life join hands
and the heavens bear the earth
through the strength
of our human speech

For in the Word is the strength
that reunites the worlds
encompasses beings
invigorates meaning and purpose

4

Earth
you are
we stand upon you
sleep into you
die right through you
and are reborn from you

The cosmos
speaks through you
through your body
to us
to our souls
within our spirit:

Stand o human being
forth from yourself
stand o human being
within yourself
as the cosmic child
whom you are from first beginnings
surrendering to the earth
to all her colours
moods
conditions
to learn
to grow
to ripen
like a seed
bearing the light of the stars
of suns

of planets
in the name of your being
and of the gods
making your way
raising
illumining
divine existence

5

O human being
be conscious of your tasks
of the responsibility you bear
as a divine being
to be the earth's guardian
her child and mother at once
for she dies in you
endowing you with life
to rise again anew in you

You wield the sword
of death and of new life
by the grace of your spiritual powers
death and life
decide
in what manner you work
in whose name you act
out of what power you live

6

Receive o human soul
the gifts of the spirit world
which bless your being
fulfil it
seek to ripen it

For all which you need
and desire
is there
your soul is rich
endowed
made able
to bear your destiny
and that of the earth
if only you affirm
your destined paths

They may lead you astray
but do not be deceived:
the truth is different
and knowledge of it
reposes in you
as the light of your soul

Kindle it
never cease
kindling it
and you will see
what rewards come
unspeakable gifts

7

Walk on
alone
your paths are not pre-ordained
it is up to you
to choose them
left or right today or tomorrow
follow your voice
it resounds
in the tones
of the god who you are

When he speaks
give him your words
accept yourself
in his light

Bibliography

Georg Friedrich Daumer, *Kaspar Hauser*, Dornach 1983

Ruth Dinesen/Helmut Müssener, *Briefe der Nelly Sachs*, Frankfurt am Main 1984

Karl Heyer, *Kaspar Hauser und das Schicksal Mitteleuropas*, Basel 1999

Franz Kafka, *Ein Landarzt und andere Drucke zu Lebzeiten*, Frankfurt am Main 2008

Novalis, *Schriften Band 2, Das philosophisch-theoretische Werk*, Munich/Vienna 1978

Kae Tempest, *Brand New Ancients*, Picador 2013

A note from the publisher

For more than a quarter of a century, **Temple Lodge Publishing** has made available new thought, ideas and research in the field of spiritual science.

Anthroposophy, as founded by Rudolf Steiner (1861-1925), is commonly known today through its practical applications, principally in education (Steiner-Waldorf schools) and agriculture (biodynamic food and wine). But behind this outer activity stands the core discipline of spiritual science, which continues to be developed and updated. True science can never be static and anthroposophy is living knowledge.

Our list features some of the best contemporary spiritual-scientific work available today, as well as introductory titles. So, visit us online at **www.templelodge.com** and join our emailing list for news on new titles.

If you feel like supporting our work, you can do so by buying our books or making a direct donation (we are a non-profit/charitable organisation).

office@templelodge.com

TEMPLE LODGE

For the finest books of Science and Spirit